WOMEN OF OKINAWA

WOMEN O

OKINAWA

NINE VOICES FROM A GARRISON ISLAND

RUTH ANN KEYSO

Afterword by Masahide Ota

Cornell University Press

Ithaca & London

First published 2000 by Cornell University Press
First printing, Cornell Paperbacks, 2000

Printed in the United States of America

Library of Congress Cataloging-in-Publication Data
Keyso, Ruth Ann, 1968–
    Women of Okinawa : nine voices from a Garrison Island / Ruth Ann Keyso;
afterword by Masahide Ota
        p. cm
    Includes bibliographical references.
    ISBN 0-8014-3788-1 (cloth : alk. paper)—ISBN 0-8014-8665-3 (paper : alk. paper)
    1. Women—Japan—Okinawa Island—Interviews. 2. Women and war—Japan—
Okinawa Island—History—20th century. 3. World War, 1939–1945—Campaigns—Japan—
Okinawa Island. 4. World War, 1939–1945—Women—Japan—Okinawa Island. I. Title.
HQ1764.O44 K48   2000
305.4'0952'294—dc21

                                                            00-008916

Cornell University Press strives to use environmentally responsible suppliers
and materials to the fullest extent possible in the publishing of its books. Such materials
include vegetable-based, low-VOC inks and acid-free papers that are recycled, totally
chlorine-free, or partly composed of nonwood fibers. Books that bear the logo of the FSC
(Forest Stewardship Council) use paper taken from forests that have been inspected
and certified as meeting the highest standards for environmental and social responsibility.
For further information, visit our website at www.cornellpress.cornell.edu.

Cloth printing   10 9 8 7 6 5 4 3 2 1
Paperback printing   10 9 8 7 6 5 4 3 2 1

CONTENTS

INTRODUCTION

I arrived in Okinawa on September 29, 1997, on a small commuter plane that had left Osaka, Japan that evening. What I remember most vividly about the flight from Japan's mainland to its southernmost prefecture was the number of U.S. servicemen on the plane, bound for one of the American military bases that crowd the island. Looking around the cabin I saw dozens of smoothly shaven heads, perfect arcs rising above the horizon of the headrests. As I listened to the young men laugh and talk in English, I felt at home, not eight thousand miles away from Levittown, Pennsylvania, and thirty thousand feet above the Pacific Ocean. The only reminder that I was on my way to Okinawa was an occasional message in Japanese over the loudspeaker announcing our arrival to the island.

At Naha International Airport I gathered my luggage and glanced around the brightly lit arrival lounge in search of an American researcher from the University of the Ryukyus, who had agreed to pick me up. The tiny airport in Okinawa's capital city was crowded that Monday night with islanders dressed in bright summer shirts and sandals, and U.S. Marines clad in heavy camouflage pants and shiny black boots.

I squeezed through the pockets of people and headed toward the phones at the far end of the lobby, unwieldy camera equipment dangling from my shoulder, an overstuffed rucksack drooping off my back. When I stopped for a breather, I was approached by a marine wearing starched fatigues and a stiff expression. "Ma'am," he asked. "Are you going to base? The bus is waiting." I told him I was a civilian and waiting for an acquaintance to pick me up. The look of confusion on his face was one I would encounter often during my year on the island. "If you aren't with the military," both Okinawans and Americans would ask me, "what are you doing on Okinawa?"

I journeyed to Okinawa, the largest and most populous of Japan's Ryukyu Islands,[1] to write a history of the island's postwar past — the recent past as the women of the island remembered it. The project wasn't an academic obligation or a longtime dream. Rather, it was something I felt inspired to do by a University of Michigan graduate course on the anthropology of the Ryukyu Islands. Dr. Teigo Yoshida, a visiting professor from Tokyo University, taught the course. Dr. Yoshida's enthusiasm for Okinawa — its religion, its people, its history — ignited my own interest in the island.

Japan was a familiar place. After having graduated from the University of Notre Dame in 1991, I spent three years in Ibaraki Prefecture — about two hours north of Tokyo — teaching English on the Japan Exchange and Teaching Programme (JET), sponsored by the Japanese Ministry of Education. I loved Japan, and my stay fueled my desire to study the language, history, and politics of the country formally. In 1995, I returned to the United States and enrolled in the Center for Japanese Studies at the University of Michigan, where I earned my master's degree two years later. In the fall of 1997, with a fellowship from the Ito Foundation for International Education Exchange, I traveled to Okinawa to begin researching the island's postwar history.

What I knew about Okinawa concerned the last major battle of World War II, which had destroyed the island during the spring of 1945. During eighty-two days of intense conflict between American and Japanese troops on this South Pacific island, nearly one-third of Okinawa's civilian population was killed. Some died from enemy gunfire and aerial bombings; others committed suicide, fearing capture and torture by American soldiers, whom they called "barbaric"; while still others took their lives at the behest of Japanese troops, who wanted to stretch already meager food supplies.

When the conflict ended on June 22, 1945, more than 12,000 American troops, 90,000 Japanese troops, and 125,000 Okinawan civilians were dead. Memories from this three-month-long battle continue to haunt war survivors today, more than half a century later.

My initial reaction to Okinawa was shock. The shops surrounding the U.S. military bases and lining *Kokusai Dōri* (International Street) in Naha, the island's capital, were disturbing reminders of Okinawa's past. "Surprise Attack!" one colorful sign read, luring shoppers inside with displays of military surplus items, from shiny silver dog tags to key rings and cup holders made from glinting brass bullet casings. Crowding the sidewalks in front of other stores were racks of camouflage jackets and pants and stacks of olive-green helmets, exhibits that appeared to taunt the islanders, forcing them to remember their island's wartime past. The insensitivity of those displays on an island that had suffered such heavy human losses struck me.

With this impression in mind, my original intention was to write about the lives of war survivors. I began talking with people of that generation and visiting historical sites on Okinawa — the underground headquarters of the Japanese naval forces, Mabuni Peace Park and *Himeyuri-no-tō* in the southern part of the island, the "Cave of the Virgins," where 222 Okinawan schoolgirls were mobilized during the war to work as nurses for Japanese troops.

But as time passed, my project took on a different angle. Speaking with women of various ages, I learned that the war did not represent the same things to all people. Women born during wartime had no recollection of the battle on the island, nor a perception of Americans as the enemy. Instead, they had powerful memories of Americans as occupiers, people in authority whose presence radically changed the Okinawa that their parents and grandparents recalled. These women seemed less interested in the war, more concerned with discussing the island during the 1960s and 1970s — when nationalistic feelings on the island were escalating and resentment toward the American military increasing. They were tired of the vast U.S. presence on the island, they said, and began to campaign for an end to the American Occupation and a return to Japanese rule. After all, the war was long over. Shouldn't the Americans go home?

For the young people on the island, those in their twenties and thirties, the war meant almost nothing at all. They had no recollection of the Battle of Okinawa, the subsequent American Occupation, or the island's formal return to Japan in 1972. For them it was normal to grow up on an island crowded with U.S. military troops, indelibly influenced by a foreign culture. They looked at the bases and the foreigners behind the steel fences with a sense of fascination, the war memorials with a sense of confusion. Many did not associate the vast U.S. military presence on the island with the battle that had rocked Okinawa more than half a century earlier. For them, the U.S. presence was a mainstay of Okinawan society, something that existed long before they were born and not likely to disappear.

As I explored the differences in how these women thought, I decided to expand the focus of the book to include stories from three generations of Okinawans and to chronicle how each generation made sense of the island's past. This past, I would discover, comprised not only the islanders' views of Americans but also their views of themselves, of the mainland Japanese, and of Okinawa.

My reason for concentrating on the memories of women was simple: women had had the most direct contact with American GIs over the preceding half-century. They were the ones who worked for the Americans in the postwar years — in clubs as waitresses, in stores as cashiers, and in private homes as maids. They were the ones who married GIs — some for love, others for money — and bore their children. And they were the ones who were the primary victims of sexual and other forms of physical violence committed by military personnel on the island.

Women also played a significant role during wartime in supporting their families both economically and emotionally while men fought to protect the country. And, because so many of the island's men died in battle, women were responsible for rebuilding Okinawa in the postwar years and restoring a sense of normalcy to people's lives. Women also enjoyed more status and power in the aftermath of war as democratic reforms introduced by the Occupation forces upset the male-centered order and propelled women into positions of responsibility. As family breadwinners, newly enfranchised mothers, or instructors of classical dance — previously a male-dominated occupation — women began to enjoy rights and privileges in the postwar period that were formerly unobtainable. I wanted to celebrate these women, to share with the world their amazing accomplishments and the environment in which they realized them.

The search for women to interview was not as difficult as I had imagined. Admittedly, when I first arrived on the island I feared many Okinawans would be reluctant to talk with me. After all, I am an American, from a country whose military bases cover their island. And I was requesting two- or three-hour interview sessions monthly from my sources, several of whom held full-time jobs while raising families. To my surprise and relief, the nine women interviewed were enthusiastic about the project, cooperating with my request to explore private elements of their past.

Okinawans don't hate Americans, the women tell me, despite animosity between the two groups during World War II. "I like the Americans as individuals," says Fumiko Nakamura, age 84. "It's the military I disagree with." Others say they harbor more resentment toward the mainland Japanese than they do toward the Americans. After all, they say, their island was sacrificed by the mainland Japanese during the battle in 1945 to forestall an American attack on the country's main islands. But, years after Japan's surrender, it is Okinawa that pays the price for the country's defeat in the Pacific War.

The Japanese established sovereignty over the Ryukyu Islands in the 1870s when they absorbed Okinawa and its 160 outlying islands into the framework of the Japanese state. Formerly the Ryukyu Kingdom, the archipelago is now known as Okinawa Prefecture. During the final months of World War II, Okinawa was the site of one of the most bitter and bloodiest battles of the war. It emerged from the three-month-long conflict in a shambles: farmland was decimated, building and homes were reduced to rubble, and much of the island's greenery was burned to ash.

The American military began its formal occupation of the island amidst this confusion. The American Occupation lasted 27 years, one month and 14 days. During that time the Occupation forces constructed vast military facilities throughout the island and transformed Okinawa into the "Keystone of the Pacific" — America's military stronghold in Asia.

Okinawa remained under U. S. control until 1972, when it was returned to Japan. As a result of agreements between the governments of the United States and Japan, Okinawa hosts 75 percent of U.S. troops stationed in this Asian country. As of 1998, there were fifty thousand U.S. military personnel and their dependents and forty military installations on this island of 1.3 million inhabitants. American bases take up 20 percent of an island that measures sixty-four miles long and seven miles wide.

I conducted the interviews with the women in this book in Japanese and at places they suggested — sometimes their homes, sometimes a coffee shop, a teahouse, or a McDonald's in town. Generally the interviews were private sessions, one-on-one encounters between the woman and me, but on occasion they became more public when the woman's friends, children, grandchildren, or spouse joined the conversation. I welcomed their input, which brought clarity and insight into some of the issues we were discussing.

The nine women addressed diverse topics. The oldest generation focused on the horrifying days of World War II and the maelstrom of the immediate postwar years, a time during which they struggled to rebuild their lives in an environment characterized by physical destruction and psychological malaise. They were faced not only with the humiliation of living alongside their former enemy but also with the knowledge that they needed the Americans' economic largesse to survive.

The feelings these women hold toward the U.S. military on the island are complicated. While they recall with gratitude the initial generosity and kindness of the American occupiers, they also remember with nostalgia the peace and tranquillity of the island in the years before the war. Their difficulty in reconciling these sentiments was obvious throughout our conversations. Even today, long after the conclusion of the war, they still struggle to make sense of their island's history and their own suffering as participants in Okinawa's painful past.

Junko Isa, 67, lost nearly her entire family during the Battle of Okinawa. A 14-year-old girl when the Americans landed on the beaches near her home in the central part of the island, Isa-san watched with horror as her homeland was transformed from Paradise to Gehenna, as sanity gave way to senselessness. She recalled her family's flight to safety in the spring of 1945, a southward journey during which five of the eight members — including both parents — died. Orphaned by the war, she was raised by relatives, later supporting herself by working as a maid in the home of an American military family.

When we meet for the first time, Isa-san shows me a photograph of her father. She removes the carefully wrapped black-and-white snapshot from her handbag, setting it on the table between us. The photo is the only physical evidence she has of her family, she says: everything else was destroyed in the war. She fingers the edges of the picture gingerly, as if touching the dried petals of a wedding bouquet. The photo is one of her most cherished possessions, she says softly, as she enfolds the snapshot into its tissue wrapping and tucks it away safely in her purse.

Mitsuko Inafuku, 67, remembers the immediate postwar years on Okinawa with nostalgia. She was 17 years old when she took a job in the mess hall on a U.S. military base in 1948. She recalls the American GIs as kind people, men who let her sneak a piece of cake from the mess hall from time to time; men who drove her home at night when her shift was finished.

Inafuku-san sees U.S. soldiers on the streets sometimes these days, she says, though not as much as in the past. But she's not afraid of them like some Okinawans are, despite their size and appearance. "I used to work for the Americans," she reminds me, spilling forth a few phrases in English that she still remembers. "We go back a long way."

Fumiko Nakamura, an 84-year-old filmmaker and anti-base activist, remembers Okinawa as a peaceful place, an island of pristine beauty and serenity. But the war changed all that, she says, a pained expression on her face. Now her homeland is crowded with U.S. military bases, and the former silence is broken by the roar of fighter planes and the rattle of military helicopters.

Nakamura-san and many others of her generation say the existence of the bases contributes to the island's martial atmosphere. It is a daily reminder of the pain the islanders were forced to endure more than half a century ago. For that reason, she protests fiercely for removal of the bases. She won't stop, she says, until the island is returned to the Okinawans and peace is, once again, restored.

The next generation of women in this book — those born during wartime — share different memories of their past. Unlike their elder sisters, these women have little or no recollection of the war. Instead, their stories center on life in the 1950s, '60s, and '70s, decades defined by rapid social and political changes and distinguished by a mood of nationalism on the island — a heightened sense of what it meant to be Okinawan. These women discuss their personal involvement in the storm of social, political, and artistic changes sweeping the island and speak of how this involvement shaped their character and defined their existence.

The intense struggle for equality with mainland Japan, a battle central to the reversion movement that consumed Okinawa during the 1960s, is a common theme among this generation's narratives. They express their dissatisfaction with conditions on the island following reversion; namely, the continued existence of U.S. military bases. Trivialized and ignored over the years by the mainland Japanese, these women today are eager to differentiate themselves from their mainland counterparts and to emphasize the unique elements of their lives as Okinawans.

Tatsuko Yamada, 57, a classical Okinawan dance instructor, remembers the discrimination she experienced as a university student in Tokyo during the 1960s when, as in the past, mainland Japanese looked down on Okinawans as racial and cultural inferiors. Despite these feelings of discrimination, she tells me, Okinawans continued to campaign for an end to the U.S. military occupation and a return to Japanese rule. In 1972, they got what they wished for when the island reverted to Japanese jurisdiction. But the changes the Okinawans had been hoping for — equality with the mainland and removal of the U.S. bases — did not occur. That's when we put away our *Hinomaru* (Rising Sun) flags, she says, and took pride in our identity as Okinawans once again.

In addition to political problems, social problems also plagued Okinawa during the 1960s and 1970s. As the war in Vietnam escalated, the U.S. military presence on the island skyrocketed. Nobuko Karimata, 57, remembers fights among American GIs — black against white — on the streets of town and in the bars surrounding the military bases. She also recalls the general sense of uneasiness that characterized the island at the time. Those were scary years, she tells me. And what made matters worse, she adds, was watching the U.S. servicemen get away with crimes committed against the local citizenry, prompting many Okinawans to campaign for reversion to Japan. "Can you blame us?" she asks.

Masayo Hirata, 58, recalls another consequence of the large U.S. military presence on the island in those years: an increase in pregnancies. As a social worker, Hirata-san provided support for many unwed Okinawan mothers with biracial children. The most complicated cases at the time, she says, involved women who got pregnant by GIs they barely knew, then tried to get assistance in tracking the men down. How were we supposed to help a woman who told us the man's name was Sam Houston, and he was from Texas? Hirata-san asks with exasperation.

Discussions with the youngest generation of women in this book — those ranging in age from 21 to 35 years old — evoked memories that were primarily pleasant, cheerful recollections of high school and college days and nostalgic reminiscences of courtship and romance. Though these women's individual pasts were far removed from the hardships their parents and grandparents endured, they were not free from affliction. They, too, experienced problems, albeit different ones, growing up on an island covered with military bases and heavily influenced by American culture. The results of that influence are apparent in their style, their language, and their choice of careers.

Born into a society in which the U.S. bases were firmly entrenched, these women accept the bases with a sense of inevitability. They speak casually about both their personal and professional relationships with the resident foreigners, and the positive and negative effects of that contact. They also discuss their roles as wives, mothers, and daughters and the expectations placed on them as females in contemporary Okinawan society, as they struggle to accommodate traditional female roles and their modern sensibilities.

Maiko Sunabe says she can't imagine Okinawa without the American military bases. The 21-year-old "Miss Okinawa" (prefectural beauty pageant winner, 1997–1998) sees the bases as a part of the island, a sight as natural as sugarcane fields in the spring and ruby-red *deigo* flowers in May. She can understand, though, why older Okinawans — like her grandparents — want the bases to disappear. "They remember the war," she says succinctly. Maiko-san[2] does not.

Mayumi Tengan, a 30-year-old mother of one, recalls a time when she was proud to be from Okinawa because of the large American presence on the island. As a teenager, she found the atmosphere on Okinawa — where American men who "looked like movie stars" packed the streets of the capital dressed in blue jeans and T-shirts — "romantic" and "exciting." "I hardly knew they were military personnel," she admits. "They looked like ordinary civilians."

Mayumi-san now realizes the existence of the bases on Okinawa is not as "cool" as she once thought. The U.S. military presence has caused many problems over the years, she says sadly, referring specifically to the rape of a 12-year-old girl by three U.S. servicemen in 1995 and to "countless other acts of violence against women."

Mariko Higa, 35, works on a U.S. military base. She says it bothers her when Okinawans complain about the number of bases without considering the economic advantages they bring to the island. The bases are an easy target for many people who blame the military for problems such as noise and traffic congestion, she says. But Mariko-san insists the majority of Okinawans don't pay much attention to the bases. There are too many other things for Okinawans to worry about, she relates: feeding their families, for example.

Writing this book was a wonderful challenge. Through this process I discovered that re-creating the past can be a joyful occasion, a chance for an individual to reflect on the elements that have defined her existence. I also learned that it can be painful, obliging the individual to relive memories she may have struggled for years to repress. What continually surprised me during my year on Okinawa, though, was the willingness of these women to share their recollections of the past with me. They responded to hundreds of personal questions with openness and honesty, never refusing to share their memories, never resisting the opportunity to offer opinions. They were quick to admit inconsistencies in their own ways of thinking and to explain why they held certain beliefs.

Though sometimes their narratives were sad as the women recalled the death of loved ones during battle, the loss of family land and homes to U.S. base construction projects, and the harsh discrimination they felt by the mainland Japanese, the interviews were occasions I looked forward to and cherished dearly. Nothing could compare with the look of pleasure in the women's eyes when they remembered a precious moment they had not recalled for decades. They surprised themselves with their own memories, reminiscences that mentally catapulted them back to a moment in time, a private instant during which they saw themselves, once again, as a 17-year-old ballerina, a 20-year-old girl working on a U.S. military base, or a 28-year-old bride of a handsome American.

I hope that those who read this book will gain a deeper understanding of Okinawa and the people who reside there; will learn something about the island's postwar history; and will come to appreciate the joys, sorrows, sufferings, and delights that Okinawan women have experienced. I also hope that the book will inspire readers to reflect on people who have lived as victims of war, subjects of foreign occupation, and citizens of a society still shaped by a vast military presence.

In conclusion, I dedicate this book to you, the Okinawan women who joined me in my effort to document the living history of an island to which I claim no lineal or ethnic connection, but one which holds for me an inexplicable intrigue, fascination, and allure. Thank you for sharing your history with me.

THE WARTIME
GENERATION

1 : JUNKO ISA

The A&W Restaurant on Route 330 in central Okinawa was crowded one Saturday afternoon in October with gaggles of junior high school students and groups of senior citizens. Adolescent girls in navy blue sailor-suit school uniforms and tiny white ankle socks squeezed into booths against the wall, chatting excitedly about some happening at school. They paused periodically to bite into greasy burgers and gulp root beer from frosty mugs decorated with the restaurant's trademark orange-and-brown logo. The older patrons sipped hot coffee in solitude, pretending not to hear the school girls' gossip. Some leafed through their newspapers, slowly turning the thin pages from left to right as their eyes scanned the rows of vertical symbols for a topic of interest. Occasionally they glanced up to watch the young waitresses with straight black pony-tails buzz by offering free refills on root beer.

I sat in a booth against the window at the far end of the restaurant and waited for Junko Isa to arrive. She lived in a nearby neighborhood but suggested on the phone that we meet at the A&W. "It's easier to find," she said. Isa-san and I had never met, but I was confident she would recognize me, a brown-haired, green-eyed American, among the crowd of Okinawans.

Settling back in the booth, I concentrated on reading the excerpt about her wartime experience that Isa-san wrote fifteen years ago. It was published in a book along with the stories of seventy other women who survived the horrors of the Battle of Okinawa. As I read about her experience, I feared that Isa-san would be hesitant to relive the pain she suffered fifty years ago. Might she be reluctant to discuss the harrowing details of the war with me, an American? I wondered.

Isa-san arrived at the A&W a few minutes before the appointed time of two o'clock, her warm smile melting my anxiety. She wore a black skirt, a flower-patterned blouse, and low, black rubber-soled shoes. The 67-year-old woman's hair was the color of coal, save for a few snow-white strands, which were brushed away from her forehead. Her appearance was youthful.

We exchanged greetings then walked to the counter together to order drinks. When we returned to the table, she took a seat on the plastic bench across from me, setting down her heavy black handbag with a look of relief. We made small talk for a while before she admitted:

"I never thought I'd be sitting here talking about my life with an American." She laughed nervously. "Really, I kept my war experiences to myself for the longest time. Too difficult to talk about everything that had happened here on the island. In fact," she sighed, "It's hard to believe that already fifty years have passed." Her voice trailed off.

Junko Isa was born and raised in Kitanakagusuku Village, a quiet place located in the central part of the island. A teenager during the Battle of Okinawa, Isa-san was profoundly affected by the tragedy that claimed the lives of her parents and three siblings. During our monthly interviews she shared with me the details of her wartime experience and how those eighty-two days of horror influenced her to travel around the country speaking to students about the battle. Repeatedly reliving the experience is painful, she admits, but it is worth it if young people learn about the atrocity of war and vow to preserve peace in the future.

My father was an elementary school teacher before the war. He wasn't drafted into the army since he held a special position at the school: He was in charge of guarding the imperial portrait. In those days, each school in Okinawa had its own photograph of the Emperor and Empress and one person responsible for safeguarding it.

My father kept that portrait locked in a beautifully decorated box. When we students gathered together for school assembly, he opened the box and placed the black-and-white photograph in front of us. As a sign of respect toward the Emperor, we weren't permitted to look directly at the photo. Everyone did from time to time, but we weren't supposed to.

I'll never forget standing with the rest of the students at assembly and listening to the principal speak. Every time we heard the name *Tennō Heika* [His Majesty the Emperor] we stood up even straighter, pressing our arms tightly against our sides and staring straight ahead. *She demonstrated the pose.* Most Okinawans these days have mixed feelings about the imperial system, but back then we didn't question it. We were taught to believe in the system and respect it.

That belief led us to war. Before the Japanese military bombed Pearl Harbor in 1941, they were fighting battles all over Asia, and winning. We never dreamed Japan would lose in the end. All through the early 1940s, we heard nothing but reports about the success of our soldiers in places like the Philippines, Sumatra, and Singapore. That's why the teachers at school used to encourage us students to study so hard. "In the future you're going to be the leaders throughout East Asia!" they insisted. And so I studied, believing that one day we Japanese would occupy countries all over Asia.

I didn't understand much about the war until it reached Okinawa. That was on March 23, 1945, when U.S. planes bombed the main island. I was 14 years old at the time. I remember the morning well because it was the same day that the names of the students who were accepted into the girls' high school in Okinawa were announced in the paper. I'll never forget seeing my name there in black and white! I was really excited, but worried at the same time because I suspected the war was going to prevent me from enrolling in that school. And it did.

One week after the aerial bombing, U.S. troops landed on Okinawa. My family and I were living right here in Kitanakagusuku Village. When we heard the Americans had landed on the Sunabe coast in Chatan Town, not too far from where we were living, my father decided we should head south toward Shuri[1] where the Japanese troops were headquartered. He thought it'd be safer there. So all eight of us—my mother and father, my grandmother, my younger sister, three younger brothers, and I — hurried for the forest behind our house that night. Shortly afterward, the bombs started falling on our village. When we looked behind us, the whole place was in flames. We fled. I remember we couldn't take too many personal possessions with us. All I had were the clothes on my back. I was wearing *monpe* [women's work pants that are gathered tightly at the ankles], a long-sleeved blouse, and a kind of protective hat made from cotton. And my pockets were stuffed with dried potatoes and sugar cubes for making *imokuzu*. Do you know what *imokuzu* is? It's a starchy substance made from grated potatoes. We dry the potatoes until they turn into flakes of starch, and then dissolve the starch in water. Then we add some black [unrefined] sugar to the mixture. There were times during the war when we had to survive on *imokuzu* for weeks.

While my family was heading for safety in the southern part of the island, we kept passing people moving north. Sometimes we wondered if we were doing the right thing by traveling in the opposite direction as everyone else, but we never turned around; we kept going south. At one point along the way we met up with two old people who had been to Naha, the capital, peddling goods. We spoke with them for a while, and they told us about a cave located in a place called Sueyoshi near Shuri. "You should hide there," they recommended. So that's where we headed. When we finally arrived at the cave at six o'clock the next morning, there were already about twenty or thirty people huddled inside. We didn't mind, though; we were just so glad to sit down and rest for the first time since our departure. We'd been walking since seven o'clock [the night before]. I think we covered about 12 kilometers in total.

Life inside the cave was a living hell. It was cold, and the place smelled of urine and feces. You see, everyone had to relieve themselves inside the cave during the daytime. We couldn't go outside because bombs were exploding all around us. By the time night fell, though, it was safe to crawl out. That's when we used to search for food. We heard from the others in the cave about a rice storehouse nearby that the Japanese military had prepared. Japanese soldiers were headquartered in Shuri, so it wasn't too unusual to find a big stockpile of food there. There was a river near the cave, too, where we could draw water. We were lucky to be able to get fresh water. A friend of mine who was sheltered at another cave near Itoman[2] told me that she used to sneak out during the night to get water from a certain stream until she discovered that the stream was filled with blood from dead bodies lying nearby. Of course she didn't realize this at the time since it was dark when she crept out to get a drink.

Day after day we heard stories from the Japanese troops about how bravely they were fighting, and how they were planning to cut through to the enemy lines. From these same troops we also heard that women who'd been captured in the central areas of the island were being raped by American soldiers and that these Americans were killing children by ripping them apart at the crotch. *She pulled her fists away from each other in demonstration.* Of course these were just tall tales meant to scare us and convince us not to let ourselves be captured by the enemy. But I was still afraid to be caught. My father used to warn me about the Americans. "If they catch you, they'll do with you as they please," he used to tell me.

Not long after we fled our village, my parents heard through the grapevine that the eldest son of my grandmother's brother was on the island. He used to live with us when he was sent to Okinawa years ago from Peru to receive a Japanese education. He'd been drafted into the Japanese Air Force while he was still in school and was in charge of fixing aviation equipment. Unfortunately, all of the Japanese aircraft at Kadena[3] were destroyed in that bombing on March 23, 1945, so he was sent south with the Imperial Army. We decided to go and look for him. We heard that the Army was in a place called Yoza near Itoman. Before we left, my father packed a pot, a kettle, and any food that we had into two buckets. Then he hung these buckets on opposite ends of a wooden stick and hoisted it onto his shoulders. My mother and grandmother each carried a small amount of baggage on their heads while I toted my 5-year-old brother on my back. My 11-year-old sister carried the baby on hers. My baby brother was only 10 months old at the time. We walked aimlessly that night along a bunch of roads we'd never been on before. Each time we asked someone for directions, we got a different answer. We never ended up finding my cousin in the end. I know we were close, but we never managed to meet up. That was a shame.

The next place where we decided to stop and rest was a town called Arakaki in the southern part of the island. The fighting was really heavy there. We stayed in an abandoned house with about fifty other people since there weren't any caves in the area. I remember waking up every morning to the roar of American aircraft. One day the sound of the engines competed with the wails of a baby who'd just been born nearby. The mother had to deliver the baby by herself. It might seem strange that no one helped her, but at the time we were only concerned about saving ourselves. *She looked toward the ground, embarrassed.* We never heard a sound from the mother, so we assumed she died in childbirth. I guess the baby died as well.

We would've died, too, had my father not suggested we get out of that area as quickly as possible. While we were standing outside discussing where to go next, an enemy plane screamed through the sky, dropping black bombs. One of them hit the house we'd been staying in with all those other people. Completely demolished it. We could hear people crying out from the rubble for help, but gradually the voices disappeared. That's when we knew they were dead.

It seemed like no matter where we traveled in those days there were always showers of bullets around us. Sometimes we sought shelter from those bullets in empty houses or under trees, where we had to jostle with people around us for a place to stand. Most of the time we had no idea how many days had passed, or how many weeks it had been since we first fled our village. All we were concerned about was whether or not we'd be alive the next day. We just kept hurrying from place to place every time we heard that U.S. soldiers were approaching. We were usually able to cover only 2 kilometers of distance with every move.

I remember walking along the roads one night and seeing Japanese soldiers moving from south to north, and north to south. Seemed like no one — not even the military — knew what they were doing or where they were going. It was on this very road where we saw some of the worst sights during our trek south. Things like a baby clinging to the breast of its dead mother. Or a small group of children hovering around their dead mother crying out, *"Anma, Anma!"* ["mother" in Okinawan dialect]. We even saw a Japanese soldier who was missing both his legs, but who inched forward on his arms, dragging his torso along. *"Yoisho, yoisho,"* he heaved each time he moved forward. Then one night, an enemy flare lit up the area where we were walking, and I glanced over to find an arm hanging from a tree branch. Just below that was a decapitated body. There were body parts everywhere! In fact, there was hardly anywhere to put our feet since the road was piled high with mountains of corpses. Plus, since we were right in the middle of rainy season, the road looked like a swamp. It took us forever to slosh through those muddy puddles. After a while I became numb to the sights; I never got sick or cried when I saw such hideous scenes. And despite witnessing all of this, I still believed wholeheartedly that Japan would win the war.

My family reached a place called Itoman next. When we arrived there, my mother and the children rested in the shade while my father and grandmother went out looking for a cave. As soon as they left, a black bomb fell from the sky above us. I remember watching it descend. When it exploded, the fragments flew everywhere. My family was screaming out from the flames. I'd been hit, too, and got burns on my head and hands. But I was still able to run and seek help for the others.

I sprinted toward the mountains where I eventually ran into a few Japanese soldiers. It looked like they'd been fleeing from the bombs, too. I explained to them that my family had been hit, and I didn't know if they were alive or dead. One of the soldiers told me he'd just seen a man in the river and that maybe it was my father. The river? I thought. So, I begged the soldier to take me to that spot, and he did. I found my father there. He was burned badly and was in a daze. He said he'd been calling out our names in the midst of the flames, but couldn't locate any of us. When the fire had completely surrounded him, he jumped into the water to save himself.

We all managed to locate one another once the fires died down and the smoke cleared. My mother was really shook up after this incident and wanted to evacuate the area as soon as possible. Unfortunately my two brothers had been hit hard by shrapnel, just like my father, and weren't able to walk. My father decided the rest of us should go on without the three of them. "We'll all meet again," he managed to murmur. But my grandmother insisted on staying with my father and the boys. She didn't have the heart to leave the wounded behind unattended. Finally my grandmother convinced my mother to go on ahead with my sister, my baby brother, and me, and to leave her behind. So the four of us set out from the cave. It was the first time my family was forced to separate from one another.

I don't even know if I felt sad at the time. I mean, I was 14 years old, just a child. I didn't know what was happening. I was so worried about getting caught or dying that I don't think I had time to cry. We all simply obeyed what my father said and went our separate ways. We never saw each other again.

Isa-san paused momentarily. She gazed out the window at the vehicles that filled the parking lot of the A&W, the drivers leaning out of their car windows to shout food orders into the metal call boxes.

My mother, my sister, my baby brother, and I left the others and walked until nine o'clock that evening. That's when we stopped to rest at an abandoned house in Nashiro near the southern tip of the island. I remember we didn't say a word to one another as we walked along. Sometimes my mother would say something like, "Watch out!" or "Be quiet," but we never had a conversation or anything. In fact, I thought I'd forget how to talk because I never had a chance to do so at the time.

Things didn't get easier for us in Nashiro. The very next morning I got hit in the ankle by a shrapnel fragment from a gun that had fired on the house. Up until that point I'd been really strong, but suddenly I began to deteriorate physically. That night I told my mother to take the kids and go on without me. She wouldn't do it, though. She urged me to try to walk on the ankle, reminding me that up until now I had had such a will to live. "How can you give up now? Come on, let's go!" she encouraged me. So I grabbed a stick to use as a cane and hobbled along behind them. We walked through the darkness, each painful step keeping me awake.

At six o'clock in the morning we arrived in Kyanmisaki[4] where we found a makeshift cave on the premises of a burned down house. At last the four of us could sit down! In the evening after the bombing stopped, my mother went outside to wash the baby's diapers. Then she fetched some water in the kettle and mixed the potato starch with sugar before dissolving it in the water. Because of our insufficient diet, my mother's natural supply of milk had dried up and the baby, too, had to eat *imokuzu* just like the rest of us. The poor thing was so skinny you could count all his bones. And he was so weak he didn't even have the energy to cry.

Two or three days later, my mother went out again to wash some diapers. Seconds after she stepped outside we heard a blast. She'd been hit by flying fragments from a bomb and had fallen to the ground! For some reason I was paralyzed; I couldn't jump up and run toward her. I just screamed for her. "*Okāsan!*" I cried out. But she didn't answer. I thought she was dead.

You can imagine how shocked I was, then, when she stumbled through the front door minutes later! When I looked at her, I could see that she was wounded in three places on her head and shoulders. Blood was pouring out from all over her. I ran to get some water. I remember the grass and trees all around me were still burning from the blast. I hurried down the small white path leading to a well near the ocean, and when I arrived at the coastline, all I could see were black enemy boats in the sea. About fifteen hundred big black ships surrounded the area. There was no space between them; it looked like one huge black mass. Fortunately no one shot at me while I was drawing water from the well. The Americans must've had binoculars and could see that I was a civilian, not a soldier. Even though I wasn't really in any danger, it was the first time I truly felt like I was going to die. How could we possibly escape from here? I wondered.

When I returned to the house with the water, three Japanese soldiers approached me. They'd been hiding in the water tank next to the house. They said they were moving on and suggested that my mother, my sister, the baby, and I hide in the tank. Had we surrendered? I wondered. I remember thinking it was really nice of them to let us hide in the water tank. It seemed like a safer place than our previous shelter. I know a lot of Okinawans had problems with the Japanese soldiers during the war, but I was always treated pretty well by them. I'd heard stories of civilians being forced out of caves by the Japanese military and of people who had to give up their food to the soldiers, who claimed they needed it to keep their strength up. Fortunately, though, the Japanese soldiers I had contact with during the war were kind.

My mother's physical condition gradually got worse. Her wounds were already infected, and there were maggots crawling around in them. It looked like she was in a lot of pain. I wanted to do something to help her, but I couldn't even walk on that ankle of mine. So the four of us just remained where we were. We were pretty helpless.

The next morning was unusually quiet. I remember my mother didn't have the same look of pain on her face as before. She was just sitting there in the water tank talking to herself. She never snapped out of that state. Then, at about eight o'clock that morning, she told my sister and me that it was time for all of us to take a nap together. We did as she said and lay down side by side.

A few hours later I woke up to discover that my mother's body was already cold. I shook my sister awake and said simply, "*Okāsan wa shinda no yo.*"

[Mom died]. She started crying. Strangely, I didn't shed a tear. I got some water, mixed it with potato starch and sugar, and then the three of us — my sister, my baby brother, and I — drank it. I wrapped my mother in a blanket, and we stayed like that next to her dead body for two days.

When I spotted a man from the village outside digging a hole to put the dead bodies of his family members in, I approached him and begged him to let me put my mother's body in the same grave. He wouldn't do it. So there I stood next to her corpse, and, for the first time, I started to cry. I looked toward her body and said, "I'm sorry." This caused my sister to start crying as well. The baby didn't make a sound.

That evening three American soldiers brandishing weapons arrived and forced us out of our hiding place. "*Dete koi!*" [Get out of there!] they called out in Japanese. They pointed their guns right at us, straight toward our chests! I couldn't believe how big these guys were. All I remember thinking was, "Oh, my goodness, this is the enemy!" Can you imagine how I felt being lifted up by one of them and taken away in a truck? I couldn't speak or understand English, so I had to tell them with hand gestures that I couldn't walk. They nodded and prepared two bamboo baskets, one for carrying me, and the other for my baby brother. My sister was able to walk. I remember the American soldiers tried to offer us some chocolate and water, but I wouldn't let my sister take any. I thought for sure that anything given to us by the Americans must have poison in it. When I refused, the soldiers ate some of the chocolate just to show me it was OK. When I saw they didn't get sick and die from it, I figured it was safe for us to eat the chocolate, too.

The Americans transported me to a field hospital up north in Kushi near Nago City to fix my ankle. Then they took my sister and baby brother to an orphanage. While I was in the hospital, the pain in my right ankle where the fragment had been lodged gradually disappeared, thanks to the treatment I was getting. I was lucky. The whole time I was recovering at the field hospital, though, I couldn't stop thinking about my sister and baby brother. Where exactly had the Americans taken them? Were they alive? Then one day I had my first visitor. It was my aunt. She heard that I'd been taken to this hospital and came to see when I'd be released. When she came back a few weeks later to take me home with her, she confirmed that my sister and baby brother had been sent to an orphanage. Apparently my grandmother's younger brother from Gushikawa City[5] had gone there looking for them, and he didn't even recognize my sister when he saw her because all of her hair had been cut off! She looked like a boy, he said. You see, during the war we couldn't wash, so naturally our hair collected lice. I hadn't had a bath in a full four months!

Well, even though my great uncle didn't recognize my sister, she recognized him. She assured the nurses that he was her relative, and they permitted her to go home with him. My sister and I never lived together again. Seems strange that natural siblings were separated, but we had to live with whomever had the room to take us in. As for my baby brother, my sister told me he'd been placed in a separate room in the orphanage. On her second day there, she went to the room where the babies were kept to check on him, but he was gone. To this day we don't know what happened to him. I wonder sometimes if he's alive or dead. Did someone adopt him? Did he die of malnutrition? I don't know. But I'd like to believe that he lived.

Isa-san sipped her root beer silently for several moments. Then she continued our discussion, this time focusing on her life in the immediate postwar years.

Conditions here on Okinawa after the war weren't much better than during wartime. We had some food, though, thanks to the distribution of goods by the American military. I remember the GIs handing out rations like canned corned beef and Spam. We Okinawans weren't used to food like that, but we ate it without complaint. We were hungry.

After the war, I lived with my uncle and some relatives in Kitanakagusuku, the village where I was raised. Then I started going back to school again in Gushikawa City. Education was free since it was sponsored by the Americans. I remember living in a tent at school with the other students for about two and a half years. Then, just six months before graduation, we had to start paying tuition at this school. That's when I dropped out. My uncle told me he couldn't afford to pay for my schooling anymore. After all, he had sons he needed to take care of. So I had to look for a job. That's when I started working for the Americans.

My job wasn't one of the glamorous ones. I wanted to work at the PX [post exchange], or in one of the shops or clubs on base, but those jobs were already snatched up by the really pretty girls. I used to watch them heading out to work wearing lipstick and all sorts of makeup. I didn't get one of those positions on base, so I had to settle for a job as a maid. I was 18 years old at the time.

The family I worked for lived on base housing in Awase [a region of central Okinawa]. I think the father was with the U.S. Army. It was really hard being a live-in maid at their house. I did everything there: started the coffee at six in the morning, sorted the laundry, washed the dishes. I never ate with the family, though; I took my meals in the kitchen by myself. There was always enough food as I remember since the family could get American goods at the commissary on base. I guess the toughest thing about living with that family was communicating with them. See, I couldn't speak English very well at the time. I mean, I had studied it at school a little bit, but I

THE WARTIME GENERATION

could hardly understand a word the family was saying. The parents used to have to point to things when explaining what they wanted me to do. And the mother watched everything! I was so nervous about making a mistake in front of her.

There were two children in that family named Janet and Greg. They were little at the time, maybe 3 or 4 years old. I didn't look after them since the mother was usually home to take care of them. I don't remember too much else about that family. Oh, I think they may have given me some clothing since I didn't have any. They saw me sewing things for myself in the house. We were able to get old military clothing, so I used to cut that apart and make blouses.

I stayed at that job for a total of four months before another position as a maid opened up at a distant relative's house. The head of the house was a doctor. I had to go there to help him out because he couldn't find anyone else to do the job. See, most Okinawans at the time preferred to work on base because the jobs there in the stores and at the clubs were easy. Plus, the salaries were pretty high compared with other sorts of work in town.

I hated that second maid job. The doctor had two daughters who were close to my age and who didn't seem to have a care in the world. One was an elementary school teacher, and the other was a high school student. And there I was working as their maid! I did that job for about three years. When the younger of the two daughters got accepted to a trade school in Tokyo to study fashion, I cried. I remember going out back to the field behind the house and staring up at the moon and screaming at it. "Why did I live? Why did I have to grow up under these conditions?" All I wanted in my life was to go to school, and if my parents had lived I would've been able to do that, just like these two.

When I eventually left that job, I started working as a waitress in a Chinese restaurant on Kadena Air Base. I was 22 years old then. The restaurant was pretty nice, and the tips weren't bad. I remember the base provided transportation for all the Okinawan girls who worked there since none of us had cars, and it was too far to walk. An American GI used to drive around to the villages in a big truck picking up the girls for work. Then he took us home again each night.

Since I was working on a U.S. base, the thought of marrying an American man crossed my mind from time to time. But, of course, I never married a GI. My relatives would've been opposed to that, and I didn't want to be cut off from the only family I had. So I ended up marrying an Okinawan man whom a friend of my aunt's introduced me to. I guess it was like *omiai* [arranged marriage].

My husband and I didn't stay together very long after we were married. Just about a year and a half. That's because I took off! *She laughed, covering her mouth with her hand.* See, my husband's mother wasn't a very nice person. A bit on the cold side. And she and my husband didn't get along very well. There was always so much tension in the house. I tried to tolerate it, but it was just too much for me after a while. Finally, I packed up my things in a *furoshiki* [a special scarf for wrapping goods] and went to the house of some relatives who ran a restaurant. I lived with them for about a year, earning my keep as a waitress in their restaurant. My husband tried to come and see me a few times, but my male relatives wouldn't let him in.

Then, in 1958, I received my father's pension money from the Japanese government. I used that to attend beauty school in Tokyo. Okinawa was under U.S. occupation at the time, so I needed a passport to get to the mainland. We could get passports fairly easily for school-related purposes. I moved to Tokyo with two of my friends where we found an apartment and started studying.

Those three years in Tokyo were the best! My friends and I were always cooking together and going out on the town. We lived in the capital around the time Michiko [the current Empress] married the Crown Prince [the current Emperor]. I wasn't too caught up in the lives of the royals, but the fact that Michiko was a commoner was something unprecedented, so almost everybody in Japan showed some interest in their wedding.

I stayed in Tokyo until I was 30, then returned to Okinawa to work in my friend's mother's beauty shop in Naha. It wasn't long before my husband came looking for me there. He must've heard from someone that I was working in the city. We hadn't seen each other in years! Anyhow, he told me his mother had died and he had money in case I wanted to start a beauty shop of my own. I had been dreaming about having my own shop for a while.

So that's what we did. I ran the shop in Naha until I got pregnant and had to quit work to have the baby. I didn't have any relatives in the area who could help me with child care, so I had to do it myself. That's when my husband and I decided to move back to Kitanakagusuku, the village where we were from. There was also another reason for going back: my husband had to take care of the *ihai* [mortuary tablets] on which his ancestors' names were written. This responsibility traditionally belongs to males in Okinawa. So we went home because of these obligations.

I guess I spent the rest of my life as a housewife. I had two children — two boys — and I raised them at home. My husband worked on an oil tanker, so he was gone a lot on trips to Arabia. He's at home quite a bit now, though. He doesn't do anything these days. Nothing but jog and take care of our garden. He likes to take walks, too. Often he asks me to go with him, but I can't walk very far because this ankle injury still bothers me. My war wound. And if I stand for a long time on it, it hurts. In the winter, too, it can be painful.

Isa-san glanced toward the book on the table, the one I was reading while I waited for her to arrive at the A&W that afternoon.

So, you've read my memoir of the war? Writing an excerpt for that book was one of the hardest things I've ever had to do in my life. Back in 1983, the *Fujin Rengōkai* [Okinawa Women's Association] decided to gather together the stories of women war survivors and compile them into a book. That's when they asked me to write about my personal experience during wartime. To be honest, I didn't want to write about it, but I felt like I had to because I was asked. It had been years since I'd thought about the war. And I never told anyone about my experience in great detail like I was requested to do now.

I was a wreck! It took me two weeks to write everything down. It's difficult to look back on your life thirty years later and write about what you experienced. It requires a lot of thought. I remember writing a little then breaking into tears. I couldn't continue. Yet I knew I had to. So I picked up my pen again. Every time I set it down, I felt like I should be writing. So I just kept writing and crying until I finally finished it.

After that, lots of people started to ask me to speak at high schools in an effort to educate students about the war. So I've been to mainland Japan dozens of times with groups from around here giving talks about the war. And lots of groups have come here, too. You see, students in our country don't learn much about the war, especially the Battle of Okinawa, in history class. Everything about Japan's militarism is just glossed over. But I feel a special duty to teach them all about the war since one of its most ferocious battles was fought right here on the island. Sometimes the visitors from the mainland request a tour of all of the places where my family and I sought shelter during the war. It's a lot for me mentally and physically to do those tours since I have to relive all of my experiences. But it's worth it if the students learn something. I want them to understand that war isn't the way to solve problems. Look at the past. Look at what I had to go through. Do you want this to happen to others in the future? These are the types of things I want young people to think about.

After I tell the students about my experience, I usually hold a question-and-answer session. Someone asked me once why women let their husbands, fathers, and brothers go off to war in those days. "Couldn't you stop them?" the student asked me. What people these days don't understand is the intolerance of the Japanese government at the time. If we had refused to let our men go, or if the men themselves had declined service in the imperial forces, we risked being shot. But kids these days don't understand things like that. It's hard to comprehend war when you haven't lived through it.

Nowadays when I look at all the military bases on the island, it seems like we Okinawans support war. Whenever American planes left here in the past for places like Vietnam or the Persian Gulf, we Okinawans felt like we were a part of those missions because the planes took off from our island. I remember the skies here were clogged with military helicopters and airplanes during the 1960s. It was always so noisy! When I heard the roar of the planes I couldn't help but think about my own wartime experience. I just knew that others were undergoing a similar situation in another country, and that made me feel terrible.

It's funny, but I feel like my way of thinking is a bit inconsistent. I mean, I'm against the existence of the military bases here, but I have to admit there were some advantages to having the U.S. presence on the island. After all, we women got the right to vote under the American Occupation. That was a good thing. I think a lot of Okinawans feel the same way I do. It's hard to be 100 percent for or against anything here. Maybe that's difficult for outsiders to understand, but that's the reality in Okinawa.

Isa-san sat back in her chair and folded her hands neatly on her lap before continuing, the tone of her voice optimistic.

You know, these days I never think about dying. I only think about living and doing as much as I can. Maybe that's because I was faced with death so much during those wartime years. I'm not sure. All I know is that I want to enjoy the rest of my life. I'm 67 years old and really independent! I'm not afraid to go anywhere. My sons laugh at me. They say that as long as I have my legs and my lips I can survive anywhere. *She tilted her head back and laughed easily.* You know what I'd like to do if I could do anything? I'd take a trip around the world! I've already been to England, Paris, Holland, Belgium, Switzerland, Hong Kong, Singapore, and the United States. Switzerland is my favorite. It's beautiful there. I guess I'd like to see Canada and Australia next. *She eyed her mug of root beer on the table and leaned toward the straw.* Yes, *she reconfirmed as she took a long sip of the sweet, brown liquid,* that's what I would do if I could do anything.

2 : MITSUKO INAFUKU

"Do you like goya?" *Mitsuko Inafuku asked me one afternoon at our classical dance lesson. We were standing near the metal fold-up table drinking coffee and nibbling sesame cookies. It was break time, a moment to relax before proceeding with the second half of the session.*

"What's goya?" *I asked.*

"Oh, it's the most famous Okinawan vegetable!" she answered with surprise. "You haven't tasted it yet? Well, I'll just have to make it for you. Why don't we have it when you come to my house next week? I'm warning you, though," she added as she set down her plastic coffee cup. "It's bitter."

Our dance instructor called us back to resume our routine to the slow music of the sanshin, *a traditional three-stringed Okinawan instrument resembling a banjo. The twelve of us lined up in formation then began moving, stepping first right then left, sliding our feet slowly across the tiled floor to the rhythm of the Ryukyuan music.*

When our two-hour dance class was finished, we removed the white tabi [1] *from our feet, folded up our gold fans, and packed away our red-and-black wooden rhythm blocks.*

"See you next Tuesday!" Inafuku-san called out after me as she ran to catch her bus.

I rode my bicycle to her home the following week. She had drawn me a careful diagram in pencil that identified myriad landmarks along the way, from the banana fields near the roadside to the steely mirrors positioned at each sharp curve of the crooked road leading toward her home.

Mitsuko Inafuku owns a two-story house in Nishihara Town near Ryukyu University. She lives on the first floor while her two sons and their families occupy the second floor. Climbing the white staircase leading to the front door, I found the 67-year-old waiting to greet me in the genkan, *or entrance hall, of her home. As always, her round face was carefully powdered, and her black hair tied back beautifully in a doughnut-shaped bun.*

"Come on in," she called out cheerfully. I entered the vestibule and removed my shoes. She provided me with a pair of soft pink slippers to wear inside. Her house was immaculate, a grand structure with both Western-style carpeted rooms and Japanese-style tatami ones, the perimeter of the tightly woven straw mats adorned with heavy gold stitching. The shelves and tables of her home were crowded with home-made ceramic vases and pottery. She directed me toward the living room and urged me to sit down. "Now let me get that goya!" *she announced as she hurried to the kitchen.*

We sat seiza *style around the coffee table, our legs folded neatly under our bodies, as we ate lunch and discussed Inafuku-san's life in Okinawa during the postwar years. Before beginning our conversation she announced, "I have a lot to tell you about life here after the war, but first I have to share a little with you about life during wartime. If you don't understand the conditions beforehand, it's hard to understand what we experienced in the aftermath."*

Inafuku-san entertained me with stories about her work experiences, from her position as a young girl laboring in a bullet factory in Osaka[2] during the prewar years, to her job in the mess hall on one of the U.S. military bases in the late 1940s. She also shared with me her impressions of how life on Okinawa has changed over the past fifty years and her personal feelings regarding those changes. As I listened to Inafuku-san's story, I was amazed at her optimism; the way in which she made the most arduous of experiences seem more like a spirited adventure than an agonizing ordeal. Throughout our conversation she spoke slowly, inquiring periodically if I understood everything she was saying. When she got excited about a topic, she broke into Okinawan dialect. I had to stop her, reminding her that I don't understand a word of the dialect. Then she laughed, the same contagious laugh I heard at dance class each Thursday afternoon. "Let me try

THE WARTIME GENERATION

that again," she would say to me, repeating her comment in standard Japanese.

I was in Osaka during wartime. Life there was tough. I worked at a bullet factory for one and a half years before Japan surrendered. In fact, that's probably why we lost the war! I had no idea what I was doing. All of the girls in my school were summoned to work at the factory. You know, to support the war effort. We were around 15 or 16 years old at the time. We worked under bright lights and directly next to machines that made the most horrific noises. Those machines could be really dangerous. In fact, one day a girl was killed after getting her long hair caught in one. I didn't have the stomach to go over and look at the site of that accident like a lot of students did. All I remember is that after that we had to tie our hair back while we were on the job.

There were some boys employed at the factory, too. They were the ones who were rejected by the army because they were too short. Those guys never did a thing. Every time I glanced over at them, they were making rings or earrings or brooches for their girlfriends out of the stainless steel we were supposed to be using to make bullets. When I saw them fooling around like that on the job, I knew we were doomed as a country! When the *kenpei* [military police] came by to inspect our progress, the boys pretended like they were working. That was the only time they did anything. Of course I never said a word to the *kenpei* about them. I didn't want to get the boys into trouble.

When the military police came to the factory for inspections, I was in charge of getting everyone lined up outside and ready to greet them. I'll never forget the way those men marched toward us, their big swords swinging from their sides. As they approached I shouted, "*Kashira migi!*" [Heads right!], and everyone in my group turned toward the right and faced the *kenpei*. *She demonstrated the action.* Then I announced how many people were present in the group that day and how many were absent. Finally I called out, "*Kashira naore!*" [Face front!] before we filed back into the factory to work.

Our workday was ten hours long. It was always dark by the time we went home. During those ten hours we had one break for lunch. We didn't have to pack a *bentō* [box lunch] because the factory provided something for us. The meal came in a mess tin, just like the ones the soldiers used. I wish I could tell you what we ate but, honestly, I can't remember. I do recall that it never filled the boys up, though. It was enough for me, but the guys were always hungry afterward. When we finished eating our lunches, we used to toss the metal containers toward an automated washing machine that blew hot water onto the boxes to clean them.

I was working at the factory the day Japan surrendered. It was August 15, 1945. I remember crowding around the radio with the rest of the students to listen to the Emperor announce the end of the war. Everyone thought the announcement was a joke. I didn't know what to think at the time, but I do remember believing that we Okinawans were going to be OK. It wasn't the end for us despite what everyone said about the barbaric Americans and how they were going to kill us. I had relatives at the time in Hawaii, and they always sent clothes and candy and things to us. I knew they were good people from a rich country. They wouldn't do the things the Japanese military were telling us they'd do.

I guess it shouldn't have seemed so surprising to hear the surrender announcement considering that things were burning around us like wildfire. During my walk to the factory each day, I could actually feel the heat of the road beneath my feet. It was so hot it melted the rubber soles right off my shoes. The area of the city where I was working was always targeted by American planes since most of the factories were concentrated there. In fact, one morning an enemy plane roared by and dropped a bomb right on the building where I was working! I remember racing outside to the air raid shelter. I didn't even have time to wash my hands; they were still greasy from the thick oil we used on those machines. I just wiped them off on a dirty rag then hurried outside. I remember thinking I was a pretty lucky person since I never got hurt during any of those bombings.

When I was walking home one afternoon, though, I didn't feel so lucky. That's because my entire village had been burned down. I thought for sure my mother was dead.[3] I remember running frantically around the area searching for her. When I couldn't find her anywhere, I just circled the area in a daze. That's when someone spotted me and said I should head over to the school. That was the neighborhood's designated shelter. I don't even know if the person who said that to me was a man or a woman because his face was all covered in soot. Anyhow, I followed that person's advice and went to the school. Unfortunately my mother wasn't there. By the time night fell, though, she arrived at the school looking for me! Apparently she had taken the train to Nagoya[4] early that morning to buy potatoes because there wasn't any food left in Osaka. When she returned to Osaka and saw that our village had been burned down, she thought I was dead. We were both so relieved to see one another that we cried and hugged for the longest time.

Once the war was over, my mother decided we should head back home to Okinawa. Most of our relatives had already repatriated, and we didn't want to be the last ones there in Osaka all alone. Just the two of us were left; my father had died back in 1942. When I told everyone at school that my mother and I were returning to Okinawa, they said we were crazy. Seems like everyone knew how devastated the countryside there was. After all, it was the only place in Japan that had seen ground warfare; other places had been bombed from the sky.

I guess I had mixed feelings about returning to Okinawa. I used to visit as a child during summer and winter vacations, but I never lived on the island. All I knew was that it took three days by boat to get there and that on the way the scenery looked like a picture postcard. I also remembered that there weren't any toilets or electricity on the island and that people urinated and defecated outside near the pigpens. I used to see barefoot kids with runny noses squatting next to the pigpens to relieve themselves while the pigs waited around to eat the feces. That's why people on the mainland didn't want to eat pork here. But for Okinawans, pork's a delicacy. Okinawans eat pigs' feet, too. The kids on the mainland used to tease the Okinawan kids about that. "That's disgusting. You guys eat pigs' feet!" they used to say. I was never teased directly, but I heard them say it to the others.

When my mother and I arrived back on the island, I couldn't believe it was the same place I'd visited as a child. What happened to the pine trees that used to line the roads? Where were all the houses? Everything was gone. Plus, the land my mother and father had worked so hard to buy had been confiscated by the U.S. military.

See, during the war, the U.S. military took private property throughout the island and used it to build bases. My father had purchased a plot of land in Ginowan[5] back in 1941 with money he earned from his job in Osaka. He used to send cash home to his younger brother who used it to buy the land and build a house on it. The place was huge. More than two thousand *tsubo* of land [approximately 6,600 square meters] with horse stables, a pig sty, and even one of those big stone family tombs. Well, during the war, my father's brother and his family lived in the house. When my uncle was called off to join the *bōeitai* [Home Guard],[6] his wife and children moved out of the house and evacuated to the mainland where it was safer. That's when the Japanese military took over the empty house. They stayed there until the place was hit by a bomb and completely destroyed. By the time the Americans took over the land, there was nothing left on it, just rubble. The U.S. military confiscated that plot of land and incorporated it into Futenma Marine Air Station. It might be used as a runway now. Or it could be a helicopter landing pad. Who knows? *She shrugged indifferently.*

It may seem strange that my mother didn't protest for the return of our land. Some Okinawans tried to stop the Americans who came through with bulldozers to take over people's private property. But my mother, well, she didn't make a fuss. Things were tough then. We didn't even know where our next meal was coming from. The last thing we had time to do was organize protests. So we accepted the money we were offered by the military and tried to get on with our lives. The way she looked at the situation was that Japan had lost the war, so losing the land, too, was simply a natural consequence of our country's defeat.

My mother got some money from the Occupation government at the time as compensation. The money wasn't much, that I remember, but at least it was something. My mother ran a general store for a few years after the war, and the yearly income from the store was unpredictable. But the money from the lease of the land wasn't; it came every year.

At first we thought we were just leasing the land to the Americans for a short period of time. But then the Korean War started, and the U.S. military needed more land throughout the island to expand its bases. So our lease got extended. Even today, fifty years after the war, I'm still collecting money from the lease of that land. These days the money comes from the Japanese government, though. They started taking over the payments after reversion in 1972. After reversion we made a killing on this land since the Japanese offered us a lot more money than the Americans had been giving us. That's because people here had been protesting for a long time over the meager sums the Americans were doling out. For me personally, *fukki* [Okinawa's reversion to Japan in 1972] was a good thing, at least economically speaking.

Once my mother and I got settled on Okinawa after the war, I started going back to school. I was 17 years old at the time. I hated school; the atmosphere was so wild. I remember the boys were noisy and were always hollering at each other in *hōgen* [Okinawan dialect]. Plus, they used to stomp down the hall in heavy boots the American GIs had discarded. Big, old clunky boots with buckles and zippers and all kinds of things on them. *She lifted her slippered foot in the air and tried to point out exactly where the fixtures were located.* At the time, everyone at school was outfitted in clothes and shoes from the U.S. military. The guys wore khaki-colored military pants that looked like jeans, and the girls cut the pants and made them into skirts. People were clever in those postwar years. We knew how to make something out of nothing. In fact, we even made skirts out of old parachutes. Oh, that fabric was so nice! Really silky. We used mosquito net as material, too. Of course mosquito net is a bit thin, so we girls had to make sure we were wearing underwear when we put on skirts made from that material. Then, during February when it got really cold, we cut military blankets and made overcoats. I actually owned a bunch of nice clothes that my relatives in Hawaii had sent me, but I didn't wear them too much. Can you imagine me walking around school in dresses with ribbons and bows on them while the other kids were wearing those drab clothes and big boots? I only wore the stuff from Hawaii on special occasions. I also gave a lot of it to my sister. Some of it was too young-looking for me.

I didn't stay at that high school for very long. Like I said, I didn't like the atmosphere there. So I dropped out of school and took a job on one of the U.S. military bases instead. I really wanted to work in the PX, so one day I went to the town hall to take the test the military required for employment. I was pretty good at English, so I didn't think I'd have too much of a problem. Well, the day I was at the town hall, an officer from base came in looking for an interpreter. When I heard that, I raced over to the officer and tried to convince him to hire me. He took a good look at me and decided I was too young for the job. I know I looked like a kid with that blunt haircut but, honestly, I think he just wanted to hire the girls with perms and nice shapes! *Inafuku-san laughed, covering her face with her hands.*

I never got the job at the PX so I had to settle for a position at the mess hall on Kadena Air Base. I worked there from 6:30 A.M. to about 9:00 P.M. every other day for three years. All I did was stand behind a counter and dish up food for the guys. The mess hall was divided into two areas, one part for enlisted guys and one area for officers. I always prayed they'd need me in the officers' section. Those young enlisted guys had such dirty mouths. They were always yelling "Shut up!" at one another. They scared me, to tell the truth. The officers seemed a bit calmer.

That doesn't mean the officers were less dangerous, though. Sometimes they made me nervous because they used to ask me to deliver their coffee to them in their rooms in the morning. A lot of them had private quarters attached to the mess hall. Well, I was careful when I went in there with the coffee. I never got too close to them, and I always made sure the door didn't get locked behind me. We had a system in the kitchen: If a girl was gone too long delivering coffee, we'd go looking for her. I hated to be suspicious, but there were problems sometimes when the men started grabbing the girls. Personally I never had any trouble, but some girls did. My sister was one of them.

My younger sister worked in the mess hall with me. The men called her "Smiley." They had nicknames for a lot of the girls. Mine was "Enri." My first name, Mitsuko, isn't so hard to pronounce, but they always called me Enri instead. *"Enri, Enri," she repeated with a look of confusion on her face.* Does that mean something in English? I mean, I could never figure out if it was a boy's name or a girl's name. Eventually I answered to it. But it always seemed like a funny name to call me.

One of the officers on base showed an interest in my sister, and they started dating. My sister insisted he was a good guy because he told her over and over again that he was a Christian. Well, when her stomach started getting bigger, and he took off for America, we wondered what sort of Christian he was! Turns out he was married and had kids back home. Oh, you should've heard the people in the village talk about her. "That's an American baby she's got in her stomach," they used to say. My sister eventually gave birth to a little girl and named her Tamiko. The baby's father's name was Tommy. I don't know why my sister chose a name like Tamiko that sounds like Tommy if she hated that man like she said she did.

After my sister's experience I wasn't so interested in dating any American GIs. I joked around with them at work sometimes, but if they tried to have a conversation with me I told them, "Sorry, I'm busy!" and ran away.

I guess the best thing about working in the mess hall was the chance to eat the leftover food. The other servers and I used to gather in the back where they had a special place for the Okinawans to eat. I remember having things like fried rice and ice cream. I used to overeat every time. That ice cream was delicious! And there were all sorts of it, even the pink-colored kind. We Okinawans weren't used to the calcium, though, so we got diarrhea after eating a lot of it.

It's embarrassing to admit this, but sometimes we girls even sneaked food out with us in the evenings before going home. The Americans used to warn us not to take anything from the mess hall. In fact, they even checked our *furoshiki* [large scarf used for packing and carrying articles] before we left at night. So we hid the food in the sleeves of our kimono. At the time I never thought of it as stealing. We just called the stuff we took "war booty." We even wrapped up the leftover meat from the soldiers' plates and ate it at home with our dinner. I remember taking some home to my mother once. She just fried it up with vegetables and we had a feast. I think some of the American guys knew what we were doing because every once in awhile they slipped us an extra piece of cake or something to take home at night.

I eventually stopped working at the mess hall when I got a job as a maid for an American family. I was 20 years old at the time. One day after I arrived at the mess hall for work, the sergeant in charge approached me and asked if I'd like a job as a maid in his house. He told me his wife was going to come to the mess hall to talk with me. I was pretty excited to go and work in his home. I could see the military housing units behind the barbed wire fences and always imagined it was a different world there, a dream world of sorts. It was.

My mother was against my decision to take the job as a live-in maid. She said she'd be lonely in the house by herself. I promised her I'd only stay for a week, but I ended up staying there for about a year and a half. I'll never forget stepping inside that house for the first time. There were thick carpets, soft sofas, and big appliances everywhere. The greatest sight, though, was the stack of bath towels in the bathroom closet. Towels in every color of the rainbow! *she said reverentially.* They had it made, those Americans. They even had a washing machine. That made me pretty happy since I was the one doing the laundry. I was used to scrubbing clothes in the river. Now all I had to do was put the things through a roller and watch as the machine took care of them.

My other duties included ironing and cleaning around the house. I never did the cooking, just the preparations, such as peeling the potatoes. We had potatoes with the meal every single night. I used to peel them and then cover them up and put them in the refrigerator. When the mother of the house came home, she cooked the meal.

I guess the hardest part of my job was taking care of the little boy. This American couple had one child, a 4-year-old boy named Chuckie. I used to baby-sit him during the daytime when the mother and father were at work. That kid was a terror, *she said with clenched teeth*. One day he grabbed the scissors and escaped from the house. I found him tearing through the neighborhood cutting up sheets people had left on their clotheslines to dry! The women on the block let me have it when they saw what he was doing to their laundry.

I learned a lot of English on the job because I was always yelling at that boy. "I'm gonna spank you!" I used to tell him when he locked me out of the house. At other times I warned him, "Don't fool around with us Okinawans! I'll bop you in the nose!" Then one time he asked me for some chocolate. I found a box in one of the cabinets and gave him a piece, but he kept pestering me for more. So I gave him a couple more pieces just to keep him quiet. Boy, did I regret that afterward. Turns out I had given him some of those chocolate-flavored laxatives. I couldn't read the label because it was written in English!

Even though the little boy drove me crazy, his mother was a sweet person. She tried to fit in with Okinawan society as much as possible. She always wanted to go to the market in Naha. We went there pretty often, mainly to buy eggs. We never seemed to buy anything else there, come to think of it. Seemed silly to me to go all the way to Naha to buy fifteen eggs, but she insisted the eggs from the market tasted better than the ones from the commissary.

The whole family went on those outings to Naha. I never wanted to go, but the parents needed me along to act as interpreter. The mother loved to barter with the old ladies at the market. She used to say to me in English, "Ask them to lower the price for me." Then I had to ask the old ladies in Japanese if they'd consider giving us a little discount. They used to answer me back in *hōgen*. "The price is final!" they'd say. Then I had to break the bad news to the mother. She usually ended up buying the goods anyhow.

Whenever we went to the market, the mother dressed in shorts and *geta*. Do you know what *geta* are? They're traditional Japanese sandals. It was so funny to see her clopping around in those wooden shoes while wearing a pair of short-shorts. But she could get away with it; she had a nice shape. And a pretty face. I remember she made herself up nicely. She had jars and jars of makeup lined up on her dresser, all sorts of little containers that held things like rouge and eye shadow and lipstick. One day she let me have a small makeup set filled with layers of colorful eye shadow and blush disks. I was so excited! Only I didn't know how to put any of it on. When I put it on my lids and opened my eyes, you couldn't see the shadow at all. That's because my eyes are small, not like her American eyes, which were really big. So, I tried putting the shadow under my eyes instead of on the lids. There I was in front of the mirror looking like a panda with sky-blue eye shadow under my eyes when she walked in the room. She laughed and laughed at me. "No, no, Enri. You put it on top of your eyelids!" she told me.

Sometimes on the weekends this American family drove me home to see my mother. I guess I went home about once every two months. On those occasions I always dressed up in a cute outfit they'd given me. You should've seen the faces on the people from the village when I pulled up with the Americans in their car. The kids in the neighborhood used to circle the parked car and touch it, always leaving dirty hand marks on the frame. Okinawans didn't have cars at the time; just the Americans could afford to drive.

Overall, I think the people in the neighborhood thought I was lucky to be working for the Americans. And I felt lucky, too. I always came home with *omiyage* [souvenirs or presents] for my mother, and a little money from my job that I shared with her, too. After all, I didn't have anything to spend my money on at that time. There was nothing to do for fun here. The only thing I remember doing for relaxation was sitting in the living room of the Americans' home while the mother taught me how to make lace. She could make all kinds of neat things out of it. I remember she had a vase of carnations constructed from lace in the corner of the living room. While she and I made things together, we listened to country music on the radio. That's all they seemed to play at the house, so I eventually learned to love that kind of music. Even today when I hear country music I feel nostalgic.

I stayed with that American family for about a year and a half. Then I decided to change jobs because I wanted something more challenging. That's when I took a job as a cashier at a restaurant on Camp Kuwae Marine Base. We used to do great business there. Sometimes the restaurant made more than two thousand dollars a night. Lots of people used to come in for something to eat after a boxing match or some other event on base. I was so busy ringing them up I hardly had time to look away from the register.

I worked at that restaurant until I turned 22, and then I got married. That was in 1952. I didn't have an arranged marriage, but I don't think it's fair to call it a traditional love marriage either. You see, at the time, my mother and I were living together, and sometimes things were tough without a man around the house. When a typhoon came, inevitably something blew off our house. One time it was the door. I remember my mother calling someone to come and fix it. It was a man who'd moved here from Osaka after the war to work construction. My mother knew him because he used to shop at her store all the time. Up in Osaka he worked as a *soroban* [abacus] teacher. Smart guy. He could calculate numbers so fast. I guess I grew to like him because he could do something I wanted to be able to do. We always do that, don't we? We're attracted to qualities in a person that we ourselves don't possess.

Anyhow, he came over to fix the door, and four months later my stomach started to swell. That's when we got married. We had four children together, two boys and two girls. In fact, my two sons share the upstairs of this house with their families. *She pointed toward the ceiling.* This man, the father of my children, died more than twenty years ago. We weren't together at the time. I divorced him when I found out he was running around with another woman. That was thirteen years into our marriage. Well, we had a fight one day, and he ripped up our wedding photos and some other pictures that were really special to me. Didn't I tell you about the pictures the American photographer had taken of me? That happened back when I was working in the mess hall on base. One day a photographer from the States came in with an interpreter. He said he was looking to photograph ordinary Okinawans in the immediate postwar years. He asked me if I'd pose for some pictures. I was surprised. I mean, I thought he'd want someone prettier. But he said he wanted me as his model. I was ready to refuse until I went home that day and learned that everyone in the village knew about his request. The head of our village said he thought it'd be OK for me to do it, so we went through with it. At first I was worried about what people in the village might think if I agreed to pose for those shots. Would everyone talk? Would rumors start? But since the head of the village approved the project, no one could say anything. In fact, the photographer made everyone happy by taking a shot of the whole neighborhood. You should've seen all the barefoot people in that photo.

I guess he took about twenty pictures of me in total. There was one of me getting into a military jeep, and another as I ironed clothes in the house. That was a funny one because the irons we used at the time had little spouts for steam on the top that looked like chimneys. Another shot showed my mother and me squatting in front of the stove as we placed potatoes in the oven. I almost died when I saw that photo! It was so close up you could see every hair on my arm. *She extended her left arm out in front of me.* As you can see, I don't have any hair on my arms now, but at the time I had long black hairs. And they stood out in that photo. One of my favorite shots, though, was a group photo where I was wearing a pair of high heels. I don't know what I was trying to prove in those shoes. The ankle strap fit nicely around the back of my foot, but the sole of the shoe extended a good inch behind my heel. Those shoes were entirely too big for me. But I guess I didn't have any others. I think one of the sergeants at the mess hall had given me those shoes a few years earlier.

When that American photographer returned to the States, he sent me big black-and-white copies of the shots he'd taken. I kept them wrapped up nicely, then stored them with my wedding photos after I got married. Unfortunately the father of my kids destroyed all of those memories. I'm sorry I have nothing to show you. I never told my kids about that incident. It's a shame I don't have those photos anymore.

When Inafuku-san and I met at a soba-ya, *or noodle restaurant, a few weeks later, she shared with me her thoughts about changes in Okinawan society during the postwar period. She also discussed her hopes for the island and its people in the future.*

Okinawa has been through a lot in the past fifty years. I guess what has changed most here is our standard of living. The island was really poor right after the war. It looked like Vietnam today. You've seen what Vietnam looks like on TV, right? Well, conditions here in Okinawa were similar, really poor. I remember some girls didn't even have to go to school because their parents needed them to help out around the house. You could see those girls doing their chores while they carried their baby brothers or sisters on their backs.

One of the most common chores was drawing water from the well. There weren't indoor faucets at the time. I remember seeing girls carrying buckets of well water on their heads. I never saw this on the mainland where I spent most of my childhood, but it was a common sight here. In fact, there are still women who can carry heavy loads in baskets on their heads to this day! When I went to a sports festival at one of my grandchildren's elementary schools recently, there was an event that all of the grandparents were asked to participate in. We had to line up holding a basket on our head, and then race toward the other end of the field. Then we were supposed to put tangerines in the basket and hurry back with it. Well, some of those women could carry baskets on their heads like hats! They just threw the fruit in the basket, rested the basket on top of their head, and took off. I didn't do so well. My tangerines kept falling out all over the place. Maybe if I had carried baskets on my head as a child. . . . *Her voice trailed off.*

Anyhow, Okinawa isn't such a poor place anymore. I don't think our society is a wealthy one, but we're comfortable. I'm happy.

Even though things have improved here economically speaking, we've still managed to hold onto some customs such as *moai* that were popular back when we were poor. You've heard of *moai,* right? I don't know when it came about exactly, but I know it existed in the prewar period because my mother was involved in a group. *Moai* groups are moneylending groups that were established by people as a way to help one another out financially. Sort of like a support group. They flourished in the early postwar years since it was easier to go to the *moai* members for money than to the bank. No need for an *inkan* [a wooden name stamp used for signing documents], no need to wait in long lines . . . These days most *moai* groups are formed strictly for friendship, though, not out of necessity.

Moai works like this: a small group of people gets together and decides how much money they want to wager. The group I'm involved with doesn't wager much, just ten thousand yen [approximately eighty dollars].[7] Every time we meet — usually once a month — each person puts ten thousand yen into the pot. Then we decide among ourselves who's going to take the pot of cash that month. It usually goes to someone who's strapped that month, you know, a person who has a son or a daughter getting married, or someone who needs a new refrigerator or something. If several people need the money, we draw straws to see who gets it.

When we meet the following month, everyone puts ten thousand yen into the pot again. Only this time it gets complicated because we add interest. The interest isn't too much, usually around one thousand yen. The people who pay interest are the ones who've already received the money. The ones who haven't had a turn to collect the pot of cash don't have to pay. The people who hold out until the end are the ones who make the most cash because they get all that interest along with it. No one really complains about having to pay the interest or anything, though. If we borrowed money from the bank, we'd have to pay interest anyhow, wouldn't we?

You have to be careful about doing *moai* with strangers. There've been cases when a person — usually one of the first people to take the pot of money — will run off with it instead of coming back to the *moai* group each time and anteing up. That's why I only do *moai* with people I know well. Most people here feel the same way. They do *moai* with their friends. Even though *moai* is illegal because it's like gambling, everyone still does it. Or at least they know someone who's in a *moai* group. I think *moai* will always exist in Okinawa. It's an important part of our culture.

Inafuku-san lifted her bowl of noodles and drank the broth, her loud slurps indicating appreciation for the taste.

Regarding other changes in our society, I think people these days are becoming more aware of how discriminatory Okinawan society is toward women, and are working to change that. For example, more females these days are questioning why the *totome* custom still exists here on the island. Do you know about *totome?* It's an old Okinawan tradition where a person's inheritance and the *ihai* [mortuary tablets on which the names of deceased family members are written], are passed to male offspring, generally the firstborn male son. Well, lots of people have started criticizing *totome* recently because they think women should have the right to inherit their parents' property or money, just like men. Even though there's no formal law in Okinawa validating *totome,* people still respect this custom. I guess that's because traditions are strong here on the island. But people are going to have to start thinking about passing on their inheritance to their daughters because they're having fewer children these days, and they might not even have a son. Things will probably start to change here more rapidly after my generation passes on. I don't think today's young people will continue to preserve this custom in the future. It doesn't seem realistic anymore.

In my opinion, *totome* makes men arrogant. I mean, they think they can just sit back and relax and not do a darn thing because they're the firstborn sons, or because they're the ones who'll inherit their parents' money and property. They're stuck-up, that's for sure. But that's what happens when you're treated differently from childhood, always spoiled and made to feel important and special. Female children don't enjoy the same treatment. As Okinawan women become more educated they're going to stop putting up with this inequality. We're getting tired of what we call *danson johi*. That's an

THE WARTIME GENERATION

expression that means, "Men are exalted, and women are oppressed." Pretty true here on the island, don't you think?

Even the custom of burial on Okinawa is discriminatory toward women. You've seen those turtle shell-shaped graves all around the island, haven't you? We say the shape of those tombs resembles a woman's womb.

Inafuku-san reached into her purse, retrieving a pencil and paper. Then she hastily sketched one of the kamekōbaka *[turtle shell-shaped tombs] for me.*

The dead bodies used to be piled high inside like this. *She drew a pyramid-shaped structure of coffins stacked atop one another.* Long ago we used to bury bodies, not burn them. Then once the bodies disintegrated, we washed the bones and placed them in urns. These days the bodies are burned right away.

Wives and husbands were placed next to one another inside these tombs. If a woman didn't marry, she was in a real predicament because she had nowhere to be buried. See, all males in a family are buried in the same grave. Once women marry, they're considered part of their husband's family, and so naturally they're buried in his family's tomb. But what happens to a single woman? She has nowhere to go. So her family might build her a small grave to the left of the family tomb. But that doesn't seem fair, does it? Why can't the woman's bones be placed inside the tomb with everyone else's?

Maybe this sort of discrimination is what makes us Okinawan women so strong. We're known for having a good deal of confidence and a strong sense of independence. In fact, I think that's why we women divorce if things aren't right in our marriages. Like in the case of my husband, he was running around on me with another woman. I know she was probably the one who trapped him, but still, if he wanted to be with her, then fine, he could go and be with her. I wasn't going to stick around. We Okinawan women are like that. We're patient for a while, and then we divorce once we get fed up. I don't think the women on the mainland are so strong. One of the big differences is that most women up there don't work after they get married, so they're really dependent on their husbands for money. On Okinawa, though, women have to work because salaries are a lot less here than on mainland Japan. Most Okinawan men can't support their families on one salary alone.

As far as Okinawa's future is concerned, well, whenever we think about the future of the island, we think about the military bases and how long they'll be here. Personally it's hard for me to say if I'd like to see the U.S. bases removed from the island. Like I told you, I have land on one of the bases, and if the land is returned to me, the yearly payments stop. But sometimes I think it'd be nice to see the areas of the island that are currently occupied by bases used for something else. Some people have suggested establishing international research centers in place of the bases in the future. After all, Okinawa is surrounded by Asian countries. People from those countries could come here to study Okinawa. I don't know if that'll ever happen, but I guess it doesn't hurt to dream about it, right?

Despite the problems on Okinawa, my impression of the Americans is a good one. Some Okinawans are afraid of the Americans, especially the ones who run around in their fatigues and uniforms. But I don't have a problem with that. I don't know if it's because I worked for the Americans or what, but I feel they're approachable. I like to talk with them. And I can speak a little English. After all, I had that job on base and everything. Yeah, the Americans and I go back many years.

3 : FUMIKO NAKAMURA

"Sorry to keep you waiting!" she announced apologetically, swinging open her office door and hurrying over to where I was sitting. Smiling widely and extending her hand in greeting, she introduced herself. "I'm Fumiko Nakamura."

I stood up and returned Nakamura-san's warm greeting, catching myself grinning at the 84-year-old Okinawan woman's energy and vitality. I watched as this tiny figure with a curl of silver hair peeking out from her cocoa-colored head scarf pulled out the metal chair next to mine and sat down sideways in it.

"I'm so interested in talking with you!" she said to my relief. "You know, people never seem to take much interest in the problems of Okinawa when an Okinawan talks about them, but when a foreigner does, well, more people listen. I'm glad you came to hear my story."

Her story is a fascinating one. Nakamura-san is a documentary filmmaker, author, retired teacher, and peace activist. She has been campaigning for the removal of the U.S. military bases from the island since the 1950s. Many factors have influenced her decision to dedicate her life to the promotion of peace on the island, among them memories of her own wartime experience. She shared with me aspects of that experience, including how she promoted Japan's militaristic policies as a leader of the Girls' Youth Organization in the 1930s, and in the classroom as a teacher during the 1930s and 1940s. Even today, fifty years after the conclusion of the war, she still struggles with feelings of regret over her personal role in contributing to the senseless loss of so many of the country's young men.

ι addition to her wartime memories, Nakamura-san discussed
ι̇tions on the island in the aftermath of battle, such as campaigns
ι̇build the island's school system, attempts to achieve economic par-
ith the mainland, and islandwide protests against the U.S. occu-
ι̇n. Saddened over the terms of reversion, and the lack of changes
on the island following this historic event in 1972, Nakamura-san became more determined than ever to continue her struggle for equality
with mainland Japan, beginning with a removal of the Japanese and
U.S. military installations from Okinawa.

Nakamura-san and I spoke regularly at the Okinawa Historical
Film Society headquarters where she has been working as secretary
since 1986. Her office is situated on a narrow side street in Naha, not
far from Kokusai Dōri (International Street), the major thoroughfare
of the capital's downtown area. A tiny elevator transports visitors to the
fourth floor of the white concrete building where Nakamura-san and
her assistant, Setsuko, work. The office was always the center of great ac-
tivity on Friday afternoons when we met, as dozens of people dropped
by to say hello or to consult with Nakamura-san about upcoming events
and activities occurring in Okinawa. The thin, metallic sound of the
telephone bell and the thick voice of the newspaper deliveryman who
passed by every Friday at 4:30 P.M., provided regular background noise
to our conversations.

I still remember the very first line in my Japanese reader. It began with the
words *Tennō Heika* [His Majesty the Emperor]. The book said the Emperor
was a god, and we were all his children. Well, I couldn't understand that. I
mean, how could all eighty million of us be his children? And how could I be
his child if I never met him?

I entered elementary school in 1920 when I was 7 years old. The school I
attended was located 4 kilometers from my home. When I was in first and
second grade I went to the village school — each community had one — but
when I was ready to enter third grade, I had to commute to the main school.
It was huge. Almost two thousand children in total.

There were four major events during the academic year: January 1 (New
Year's Day), February 11 (Japan Founder's Day), April 29 (*Tenchōsetsu*, the
Showa Emperor's birthday), and November 3 (the Meiji Emperor's birthday).[1] On each of these occasions, classes were canceled, but we still had to
gather at school for a special ceremony. In the prewar period we didn't have

a gym, a conference room, or any other nice place where the entire population of the school could congregate, so we removed the partition that separated the classrooms from one another and crammed all of the students inside one big room. Then we sang the *Kimigayo* [Japanese anthem] and listened to the *kyōiku chokugo* [Imperial Rescript on Education]. When the principal finished speaking, we sang the ceremonial song. I can still remember the melodies and words to those songs to this day.

At school I took subjects such as Japanese, math, geography, history, and science. I studied English for a few years, too, but English education was outlawed after 1941 when the war between the United States and Japan broke out. The Japanese government didn't want us studying the language of the enemy; they wanted us to focus our attention on *kōminka kyōiku* [good citizens' education], a set of courses designed to teach us how to become better Japanese. In other words, how to be outstanding citizens not only for the good of the country but also out of respect for the Emperor.

After elementary school I entered normal school to become a teacher. I was 14 years old at the time. I always sat in the front of the classroom so I could hear everything the teacher said, even the things he mumbled under his breath and didn't want anyone to hear. Well, one day as I headed into the room with the other girls for history class, we noticed a newspaper clipping hanging on the back wall. It was an article about three Japanese soldiers stationed in China who had sacrificed themselves — made themselves human bombs — to break through the barbed wire that the Chinese had placed throughout their country to keep the Japanese from infiltrating. That was in 1932. The soldiers' bravery was written up in all the newspapers at the time. People even called them "*heitai no kamisama*" [soldier–gods].

While we were crowded at the back of the room reading this clipping, the teacher came in. He marched to the front of the room as we scrambled to our seats. Then I heard him mutter under his breath, "What on earth will the rest of the world think of us Japanese for doing such terrible things?" He didn't say this loud enough for everyone to hear, but I caught it because I was sitting in the front of the classroom. Had the secret police overheard his remarks, they would've branded him a traitor.

After I graduated from normal school in 1933, I took my first teaching job in my hometown of Motobu Village.[2] I was 19 years old. At that time, the war in Asia was growing bigger and bigger,[3] and on the home front, we teachers had a lot of responsibilities. I remember taking some of the older students — the fifth and sixth graders — to the homes of families whose sons were off at war. We helped the families till the fields, collect firewood for their stoves, and do other chores that had gotten neglected since the young men were called off to service. In addition to these duties, we were responsible for participating in funeral processions for those who had died in battle and for taking part in town meetings where we, as leaders of the community, had to encourage people to support the war effort and work together for victory.

At school, too, there was hardly a free moment. When one of the male teachers or a former male graduate of the school was called off to war, we performed a certain ritual. All of the students and teachers gathered together to form two lines running from the entrance of the school building to the front gate near the road. Then the new soldiers walked between the two lines of people who were waving flags and holding signs wishing the men good luck in battle. I remember we all sang a special song, too, for the occasion. We sang at the top of our lungs! We held so much respect for those men who were going off to war. All the boys at the time wanted to be soldiers just like them. They couldn't wait to be draped in Japanese flags and to walk off proudly to the cheers of us patriotic citizens.

When we finished cheering on the soldiers, we filed back into the school silently. I remember returning to the teachers room on one occasion and hearing a middle-aged male instructor next to me comment on the folly of sending our young men off to war when we knew they wouldn't come back. I was so surprised to hear someone say this. I turned toward him and asked, "What would make you say such a thing! Don't you know if the military police or the secret police heard you making such remarks, you could be hauled off to prison?" He didn't respond.

We had to watch what we said in those days. Sometimes plainclothesmen rode the trains and listened in on people's conversations. If they heard someone comment that Japan looked like it was losing the war, the police would tap that person and say, "Hey, you! Get off with me at the next stop." After that, the individual would be interrogated at police headquarters. Then the police would keep an eye on him afterward. On top of all that, he'd be forced to write a letter of regret explaining the things he said, why he said them, and that he was sorry for saying them. Yes, those years were fearful ones for us. I was forever telling the students about the glories of war, glamorizing it just like the government wanted us teachers to do. Personally I was afraid of not saying those sorts of things. After all, as a schoolteacher I was responsible for being patriotic.

When we received word of our successes in battle, we Japanese were elated. But when more and more women were becoming widowed, we knew we were slowly being defeated as a country. No one had to tell us that. And no one did. Reports about the condition of our soldiers were always optimistic; we were continually reminded of how proud we should be of them.

And the government kept hurling new patriotic slogans at us, things like, *Kyokoku icchi* [National Unity!], *Jinchū hōkoku* [Do Your Best for Your Country!], *Jūgo o mamoru* [Protect the Homefront!], and *Umeyō fuyaseyō* [Reproduce and Multiply!]. Did you know that in those days the Prime Minister himself even sent a letter of commendation to women who gave birth to ten children or more? *She laughed.*

I remember trying to do whatever I could as a citizen to support the war. I even went to Naha Port to see the soldiers off. I'll never forget the leather boots and khaki-colored uniforms the officers wore. Or the image of sailors standing on a boat as it pulled away from port. *"Banzai, Banzai!"* [Hurray! Hurray!] they cried out. *She stretched her arms in front of her, then lifted them over her head in demonstration.* I was there as leader of the Girls' Youth Organization, a post I held from the time I was 15 until I turned 23. It was a group for unmarried women. We were responsible for cheering the soldiers on as they departed for the front lines or attending funerals for the ones who didn't survive. At these funerals the family had a white box in which the bones of the deceased were supposed to be contained. Japanese soldiers' remains were never shipped back here from overseas, so the families filled the boxes with stones to make it seem as if there were bones inside. There were even cases where a deceased soldier's friend would carry back a piece of his buddy's body, such as a finger, and present it to the family. And the relatives would cry in gratitude when they received such an offering. I guess they figured that any remembrance of the deceased soldier was better than nothing at all.

I also remember making comfort bags for the soldiers at the front. We young women always tried to send a care package out to someone we knew. In the letters we told the men things about home such as, "Sugarcane harvesting season has started," or "Everyone in your family is well and thinking about you." We also wrote messages like, "Fight hard for the country!" But we never told the men to die for the sake of the country.

We made *senninbari* for the soldiers, too. Do you know what *senninbari* are? They're good-luck belts made from cotton and embroidered with a thousand red stitches by a thousand different women. We used to take a piece of white cotton cloth about 30 centimeters in width and fold it in half. *Nakamura-san picked up a piece of scratch paper and folded it to illustrate her words.* Then, we put marks on the cloth, small lines running both vertically and horizontally. After that we asked women from the neighborhood, or female passersby on the street, to make a stitch along one of these lines with a strand of red thread. After each stitch they knotted the thread. This continued until one thousand different women had made a stitch in the cloth. Sometimes we let a woman make more than one stitch. For example, I had a friend back then who was born in the year of the tiger,[4] so everyone thought she was a really strong person. That's why we let her do more than one stitch. In fact, I think she made eighteen stitches in the *senninbari* because she was 18 years old at the time. Generally we presented these *senninbari* to a special person, such as a brother or an uncle or a father. The bands symbolized our hope for the man's success in war.

Nakamura-san reached for her ocha (green tea) and took a sip.

I moved away from Okinawa for the first time in 1941. That was one year after I got married. My husband was a year older than I and was from the same village up north [Motobu Village]. He didn't have to go to war because he was sickly and didn't pass the physical for acceptance into the military. Instead, he went to the mainland for university. He planned to return to Okinawa to work as a teacher after graduation, but things didn't work out that way; there weren't any openings for teachers here at the time. So he took a job with Fuji Electric in Yokohama.[5] Before I left to be with him in Yokohama, we had a small wedding at my parents' house in Okinawa. We only invited about thirty close relatives to the wedding. It was during wartime, so we couldn't overdo things; it wouldn't be right.

The war was a tough time for all of us. I was working as a teacher in Kawasaki near Tokyo when the bombs were dropped on the city. What a scare that was! In the middle of a teachers' meeting at school, we heard a huge boom outside. A bomb had hit the nearby Nihon Kokan factory, the biggest factory in Kawasaki. The whole place was in flames. We ran outside, at first thinking the noise was just artillery practice by Japanese soldiers. But when we saw the flames, we looked up toward the sky and, sure enough, there was a plane with a star on the side. That was the sign of an American aircraft. What a shock it was to see that bomber! I remember being pregnant with my first child then, and the teachers warned me not to look up at the sky; they were afraid the sight would frighten my unborn baby.

I walked home alone from school that night. It was dark, but I could still see people passing me in the other direction. Most of them were on their way home from the hospital. When I saw the bandages they were wearing, I knew they were the ones hurt from the blast to that factory. That's when I really felt like I was experiencing war. It really *is* a war, isn't it? I asked myself. It wasn't the first time, though, that I truly felt scared. That happened when the Japanese attacked Pearl Harbor, and war was formally declared. When I heard that, I shook with fear. Up until that time I'd heard about declarations of war in history class, but this was the first time I'd heard it on the radio myself. I couldn't be afraid, though. I had to continue to tell the children in my class that Japan was *isamashii* [brave and courageous]; that our soldiers were fighting heroically. I also had to encourage them to use such slogans as, "Out with the enemy!" Of course the enemy at the time was America and England. And, as a teacher I was responsible for instructing the children to respect and honor the country and the Emperor. After all, that was a part of Tennoist education.[6] I regret to this day that I had to say such things. *She looked down at the table, sadly.*

In 1944 I gave birth to my second child. That's when I had to stop teaching. When I had my first child, I was still able to work because my mother-in-law came from Okinawa to help us in Kawasaki. She lived with us and took care of the baby. But by the time I had my second child, there was no milk in Japan — not even condensed milk — so I had to stay home and nurse my baby. Every time I heard those sirens warning us of an air raid, I was terrified. I used to grab the baby and run for shelter. We could never get a full night's rest in those days because there was always an air raid.

Then on April 15, 1945, our house in Kawasaki burned down. A bomb hit the house next door, and the fire spread to our place. Nothing could be saved. I remember my husband grabbing hold of our eldest son while I cradled the baby in my arms. Then we pulled my husband's mother by the hand and ran out of the house. We had nowhere to go. There wasn't a big air-raid shelter or anything in the area. There were small ones, but nothing strong enough. So we headed toward town. People had started flocking there, so we moved in that direction, too, thinking we might be able to find a shelter to hide in. Now that I look back on things I realize we were open targets. Fortunately we were never hit.

Before our house burned down, my family was planning to go to Kyushu.[7] Lots of people were preparing evacuation routes at the time. Well, we were all set to go; we'd already packed our clothes and utensils and everything. Then the fire came. I can still see our suitcases there in the vestibule of the house, reduced to cinders. People had warned us that Kawasaki was an unsafe place, but we refused to listen. Now we owned nothing but the clothes on our backs.

We decided there wasn't much else we could do but leave that area as quickly as possible, so we boarded a train for Fujisawa in Kanagawa[8] where I had a cousin. We rented a small room at a farmhouse and stayed there from April 1945 until November of that same year. After that, we returned to Yokohama where we found lodging in barracks that the Japanese naval officers had formerly occupied. Ironic, isn't it, that those military buildings managed to survive the fires! We stayed there for almost a year until we were able to get on a boat taking us back home to Okinawa.

While we were in Yokohama, my husband had a job helping people get repatriated to Okinawa. He assisted them with the paperwork and other formalities they needed to go through before they could board one of the boats to the island. I stayed at home and took care of the children and tried to keep my family fed. There was a dumping ground nearby that the U.S. military used, and I remember walking there and gathering together some of the wooden crates their supplies had been packed in. I burned the wood, then placed a pot of seawater on top. This evaporated the water, leaving behind the salt, which was a necessity for our diet. I also combed the beach for shellfish and seaweed.

In July 1946, we were finally able to head back to Okinawa. We took a boat from Yokohama to Nagoya[9] where we stayed in an empty factory while we waited for an American ship to take us to Okinawa. That factory in Nagoya was a huge place. There was one large room that could hold about one hundred people. The room was partitioned into sections, and each family occupied one section. Of course the sections weren't very big; just enough room for us to lie down and sleep. Thankfully there was a toilet down the hall that we all shared. It was a Japanese-style one, not a Western one, so basically just a hole in the ground with porcelain surrounding it.

While we were at this factory, we had *gohan* (rice) and canned vegetables like *konbu* (kelp) and *daikon* (radish) to eat. Those items had been stored in warehouses by the Japanese military during the war. Most of it was pretty old; I remember the rice was hard. *She grimaced.* I guess we spent close to one month at that factory until the boat taking us to Okinawa showed up. I thought it would never come.

We arrived in Okinawa one week later, docking at Kitanakagusuku in the central part of the island. It's where Kubasaki High School is located now. We stayed in Quonset huts[10] at a relocation camp there. Actually I don't like to refer to those places as "relocation camps," but more like "detention camps" because we were forced to stay there. I remember the Americans provided us with food during the week we were at the camp, things like bread with jam and butter, boiled potatoes, canned goods, and tea.

I don't remember the camp being heavily patrolled by American soldiers. And I don't think it was surrounded by barbed wire or anything. It's not like there was anywhere for us to run away to, after all! I'll admit, though, we liked to sneak out into the fields to collect sugarcane from time to time. I'll never forget how good that tasted.

There wasn't much to do at the camps. We just tried to pass the time by talking with one another until we were permitted to return to our home villages. Sometimes a person from the village government office stopped by to give us news about home and about our relatives who were still living. I can't begin to tell you how excited we were to get news like that from the hometown! After all, we hadn't heard anything about the conditions in Okinawa for so long.

Then the day finally came when we were able to return to Motobu, my hometown. As we bumped along the street in the back of a U.S. military truck, I remember being shocked at how much things had changed. The roads had been widened for military use, and all along the sides of the road were hundreds of burnt-down houses, a little flame flickering inside each of them. "Gosh," I remember thinking, "Okinawa really *was* devastated during the war, wasn't it?" Then suddenly I heard the sound of a *sanshin* [traditional three-stringed Okinawan musical instrument]. I craned my neck to see a bunch of Okinawans sitting outside on the ground watching a play. In the immediate postwar period, people put on *shibai* [plays] as a way of passing the time and cheering themselves up. When I heard the sound of that *sanshin* in the midst of all the disaster, I got choked up. "At least the Okinawan spirit wasn't completely destroyed by the war," I said to myself.

As we approached my village, I started to get impatient with how slowly the truck was moving. I wanted to jump from the back of it and run toward the village where my mother would be waiting. When the truck finally stopped, I climbed out the back and yelled for my mother as loudly as I could. "*Anma! Anma!*" ["mother" in Okinawan dialect]. Just like I used to say as a child. And lots of people came running. There was no answer from my mother, though. Everyone just crowded around me and remained silent. No one knew how to tell me she had died. So I asked them directly. "She didn't survive, did she?" That's when someone ran to get my elder sister and cousins, and they told me how my mother died.

Apparently when news that the Americans had landed nearby in Nago City on April 5, 1945, reached the village, people panicked and started heading toward the mountains. My mother had already lost her sight at this point and had grown considerably weaker in the cave where she and my relatives had been hiding. She couldn't go on with everyone else, so she told them to leave and at least get the kids to safety. When things calmed down, she suggested, they could come back and get her. They agreed and left. That night my mother took her last breath in the cave all alone.

One of my aunts used her wicker trunk as a casket to bury my mother in. Then some relatives took the body away to bury it. The bombing was so heavy on the roads at the time, though, that the women in the burial procession had to turn back while the men continued walking toward the tomb where they intended to place my mother's body. They didn't burn the body, though, since the smoke from the fire would've alerted the enemy to their position.

One month later, in May 1945, the U.S. military came through with bulldozers to widen the roads. They needed to enlarge them so transport vehicles could pass by. More than twenty graves located parallel to this road were uprooted as a result of the construction. My mother's was one of them. A few of my cousins went there hoping to collect some of her bones or at least find a piece of her kimono. But the U.S. military told them their search would interfere with traffic and they should go home. So my mother's bones are still buried somewhere in the ground up there in Motobu.

Nakamura-san was silent for several minutes. She glanced down at her teacup, wrapping her fingers around the circumference of the tiny cup as if trying to warm them. When she resumed our discussion, she focused on the rebuilding of her life in Okinawa in the immediate postwar years.

When we returned to Okinawa from the mainland in 1946, it was just three months after I'd given birth to my third child. Thankfully my relatives on the island helped us get settled. They built us a small house in Motobu, nothing fancy, just a hut with a thatched roof. Then, right when we thought we could take a breather, my husband, eldest son, and mother-in-law contracted malaria. I took care of them.

First came the trembling, followed by the high fevers. The people around us told me about a certain concoction which involved boiling leaves from a pomegranate tree. Well, my mother-in-law and son got serious cases of diarrhea from it and were on the verge of death. My husband, who should've been the strongest of the three, wasn't able to move. He couldn't get up from the bed, let alone walk. I remember my son crying out to him for help, but my husband couldn't move a muscle. It broke my heart. It seemed that since my return to Okinawa I was going to lose everyone I loved. I couldn't help thinking that way.

When fall came and the weather got cooler, the sicknesses seemed to subside, but my husband still wasn't able to do much more than wake up in the morning and sleep at night. We didn't know if he was going to be able to walk again. You know, before the war we'd never heard of malaria on the island. It seemed to me just one more parting gift the war left us. It was just one more thing for us to be angry about.

In November 1946, I returned to my teaching job. After the war there weren't many teachers in Okinawa because most of the male instructors had gone off to war and hadn't survived. So, naturally I received official orders regarding my next teaching appointment right away.

I needed to find someone to watch my children once I went back to work, so I decided to go from house to house in the area asking if anyone could help me. It was embarrassing to walk around soliciting help, but I felt I had no choice. Unfortunately everyone was too busy with their own duties to look after my kids, so I ended up carrying my baby on my back to school. I remember walking home from school in the evenings and gathering whatever food I could on the way. In each of my hands I held something edible, and on my back I carried my child. It was a long thirty-five minute walk. I knew my baby was maturing healthily when I could feel his weight growing heavier everyday.

The school where I resumed teaching was a newly built log structure with a thatched roof and walls. It had a dirt floor and when it rained, the whole room got muddy. And the roof wasn't very sturdy; it could easily blow off during a typhoon. And sure enough it did. Thankfully the parents came to the rescue and helped fix it.

The parents did so much in those days to help get the schools back in order. Some of the students' fathers helped out by making desks for the children to use. Those desks were all sorts of shapes and sizes. The fathers didn't have time to construct chairs, so we had the students sit on empty ammunition boxes. Of course the children didn't have proper school attire in those years, so they used to wear baggy clothes their mothers sewed from U.S. military surplus material. I'll never forget watching them running around outside in those clothes, their bare feet stained red from the claylike ground. And to think about how good life was for them before the war! As I watched the students playing outside, I couldn't help but worry about the kind of future they'd have.

It was important for us teachers to get the students back in school as soon as possible after the war. That's why we started petitioning the American Occupation government early on for adequate school buildings and supplies for the kids. They provided us with the bare minimum: thatched roof huts with leaky roofs and mud floors. "That's the best we can do right now," they told us. They insisted they needed to think about economic issues, such as improving our daily life, before they worried about educational ones. So, we Okinawans decided to appeal to the mainland Japanese to help us out. Chōbyō Yara, the head of the *Kyōshokuiinkai* [Okinawa Teachers Association] here at the time, was determined to go to the mainland and ask people for financial assistance. He'd already written to schools on mainland Japan explaining the poor situation in Okinawa, and many people up there started collecting money to help us here on the island. Ultimately, though, the Occupation government denied him a passport to travel to Tokyo. The Americans were going to permit Yara Sensei [11] to use the money raised on the mainland to purchase supplies the schools needed, but they weren't going to allow him to travel to the mainland to collect money for improving the buildings. The Occupation government just didn't want to lose face. After all, what would the Japanese think if the Americans couldn't even provide adequate school buildings for the Okinawans?

So Yara Sensei's hands were tied. He couldn't do anything but ask each school on the island to prepare a list of supplies it needed. Most teachers wanted items like a piano or other large equipment they'd been unable to afford. Well, the schools got what they requested. I remember the children shouting, *"Banzai! Banzai!"* [Hurray!] when a piano was delivered to the school. Now can you imagine a big, shiny piano inside one of those thatched roof huts? Really, the Americans had to do something. It looked ridiculous. So they rebuilt our schools. They constructed concrete ones that wouldn't blow over during typhoon season. And they were big enough to house those glossy pianos. In the end, everyone was happy.

After the war so many things were in short supply here, including reading material. Sometimes we were lucky enough to get hold of some old magazines or pieces of newspapers. When we did, we were thrilled! One of the teachers at school even discovered a cache of books that someone had hidden in a cave and brought them to school. Those books were like nutrition after a long famine.

Lots of the teachers liked to read at night, but we didn't have electricity, so we used empty beer cans the American GIs discarded. We poured heavy oil into them, then cut up pieces of tent and ignited them for flame. Often the teachers stayed up all night wading through books and copying manuscripts. When they went to school the next morning, their faces were black from the soot the "lamps" had given off! We didn't have soap at the school since this was just another thing in short supply, so they washed their faces using plain old water. This never got all the dirt off. And we didn't have mirrors, so they had no idea what their appearance was like. Sometimes we let them walk around all day like that!

Things were tough for us here in that first decade following the war. And they didn't get any easier. Even though conditions improved economically, we still had to deal with social and political problems associated with the American Occupation.

In my opinion the Occupation was a terrible experience. I don't mean to say all of the military personnel here were bad. But the U.S. bases just grew larger and larger during those years [1945 to 1972], and more and more GIs seemed to arrive here daily, especially in the 1960s when the Vietnam War was raging. The atmosphere on Okinawa changed dramatically. Not only was our island used as a launching pad for American missions into Vietnam, it was also a playground for U.S. soldiers needing rest and relaxation from the war. There was so much crime here at that time, lots of robberies and even murders. And we couldn't even arrest any of these GIs! They just ran behind the confines of the bases, and we couldn't do a thing about it. The Okinawan police had no jurisdiction inside the U.S. military bases.

I remember holding sit-down strikes with other members of the Teachers Association in the area around Kadena Air Base. It was our way of saying we opposed the military existence here and felt it threatened us rather than protected us like it was supposed to. Every time there was an accident, such as an airplane crash or an attack against a person, we drove or bused to the base after school and surrounded it. I remember American soldiers approaching the fences with dogs in an attempt to scare us off, but we didn't budge. The B-52 bombers used to fly down really low, low enough for us to see the pilot's face. I'll never forget the roar of those planes! We used to scream up at them, "Go home Americans!" as loudly as we could. There was never any violence at these rallies, by either us or the U.S. military. It was just a chance for us Okinawans to show our dissatisfaction and discontent.

I guess the worst thing about the Occupation period was the way our human rights were violated. If we protested against the American military presence here, we risked being blacklisted. In fact, I'm sure I was on some sort of blacklist the Americans had at the time. *She smiled awkwardly.* I remember putting in an application for a passport in 1963 to go to the Japanese mainland for a seminar on teaching writing to children. I was denied the passport for no apparent reason. The Teachers Association petitioned on my behalf. "Why can't an Okinawan woman go to Osaka for academic reasons?" they asked. There didn't seem to be anything wrong with an individual woman traveling to the mainland for research purposes. I guess there was no logical way to deny me permission, so I was eventually allowed to go.

One thing about this trip to the mainland that I remember vividly was how much the people there wanted American dollars. See, dollars could be used anywhere in the world, and Japan knew this. The mainland Japanese were trying to get their hands on as much foreign currency as possible and saw Okinawa as a *doru bako* [dollar box]. I remember going to the bank in Kobe [12] one day to exchange some dollars to yen. I wanted to shop for *omiyage* [souvenirs] before returning to Okinawa. Well, when I announced my request at the bank, they took me into a private room and served me a cup of coffee as

I waited. All this for a simple twenty-dollar exchange! They were obsessed with getting hold of dollars up there.

Throughout the Occupation, the Americans were busy teaching us about democracy and tripartite government, but they didn't necessarily practice what they preached. There were two governments here at the time: the *Ryūkyū Seifu* [Government of the Ryukyu Islands] and the *America Minseifu* [American Government]. Although the Ryukyu Government comprised elected Okinawan officials, the American Government here still had the final say on which laws passed and which ones didn't. The Americans even hand-picked the Okinawans they wanted in high governmental positions.

The American Government and the Ryukyu Government shared the same office building in Naha. It was a four-story structure located right in front of the current Prefectural Government Office. *She pointed out the window in the direction of the office.* Well, the Okinawans occupied the first two stories of the building, and the Americans occupied the third and fourth floors. The Americans even installed an elevator to transport themselves up to these floors. I don't know of any other building at the time that had an elevator in it. It was unheard of. Plus, the third and fourth floors were equipped with heaters and air conditioners. The first and second floors had nothing. There was even a helicopter-landing pad on the roof of the building.[13]

Do you know where Route 58 is? Well, it used to be called Route 1 during the Occupation years. At that time, American military vehicles were given priority on the road. Okinawans in private cars or taxis weren't allowed to pass American vehicles. If we overtook them on the road, we were stopped and reprimanded. So we had to ride in the wake of their oily exhaust fumes until the trucks steered into Kadena Air Base or wherever they were going. Then we could finally zip by!

Gradually we Okinawans started to get fed up with the behavior of the American occupiers here. I guess that's why we were looking forward to re-version to Japan in 1972. We thought our problems would go away after we were reunited with the mainland. But, unfortunately, reunion with Japan was only the beginning of more problems.

Reversion took place on May 15, 1972. It was one of the saddest days in our island's history. That might seem like a strange thing to say since I've talked about how much we wanted to return to the motherland in the postwar period. But we Okinawans thought reversion would bring with it a removal of the military bases from the island and equality with the mainland in terms of the standard of living. It brought neither.

I was so excited for the 15th of May. We Okinawans had been planning to decorate the streets with lanterns or flags, something to visually celebrate our return to the motherland. But when the 15th rolled around, things didn't feel very celebratory on the island. We discovered that conditions weren't going to change here at all. It was a pitiful situation. Our parades of celebration turned into processions of protest.

It was sort of symbolic that day, too, that it rained so hard. The drops were this big. *She made a circle with the thumb and forefinger of her right hand.* The rain pelted us relentlessly. My tears mixed with the rain until I couldn't tell which was which after a while. And my shoes were soaked! I remember how they squished as I walked along the street with the others. For us Okinawans, that day was one of the saddest days in our history. But up in Tokyo, it was a day of celebration. The people there saw reversion as a political victory.

Something that caused panic here around the time of reversion was the exchange rate we received when we converted our dollars into Japanese yen. Right after the war we used a special currency on Okinawa called "B yen," and then in 1958, we started using American dollars. The Japanese government led us to believe we'd receive an exchange rate of 360 yen to the dollar after reversion, but in the end we only got 305 yen to the dollar. Because of this, prices here went up dramatically. We heard about this poor exchange rate only a few days before reversion on the 15th. Well, the announcement caused a panic. People started running to stores to stock up on everything they could. I remember seeing people coming out of grocery stores carrying crates filled with instant coffee and canned goods. Everyone was worried about their livelihood after reversion. The head of the Okinawa Women's Association at the time, Etsu Miyazato, even stood in front of stores with a megaphone requesting shoppers not to buy up everything.

Shortly before reversion, Miyazato-san traveled to Tokyo to consult with Prime Minister Sato about the anxiety people were feeling over reuniting with mainland Japan. Many people wanted to make sure they'd receive a favorable exchange rate of 360 yen to the dollar like they were told. Prime Minister Sato assured her the Okinawans didn't need to worry about the exchange rate; the government wasn't going to take advantage of them. Well, he never kept that promise.

Naturally reversion brought about an influx of Japanese stores to the island. When we heard that the Japanese were going to construct large grocery and department stores here after 1972, we knew this would put the small mom-and-pop stores on the island out of business. The people who were especially concerned about this change were the women who worked in the market in downtown Naha. After the war, hundreds of newly widowed women flocked to the capital to sell handmade goods, vegetables, and fruit. This was the beginning of the market near *Kokusai Dōri* [International Street] that exists today. So, in an effort to preserve the livelihood of these women, Okinawans banded together and appealed to the management of these big stores to postpone their grand openings for about one year. This would give us time to come up with a solution to the problem.

Eventually we asked the management if they'd consider operating their stores at half the size they originally planned and if they'd allot some space in their buildings for local merchants to sell their wares. We also requested they employ as many local hires as possible. The stores agreed to our requests by postponing their opening by seven months and by allotting space to these vendors. This situation continued for a few years, until some of the merchants returned to the market where many Okinawans preferred to shop. They liked the friendly service and rapport between the vendors and the buyers better than the artificiality of the department store atmosphere.

Japanese construction companies, too, decided to do business on Okinawa at the time. About two or three years before reversion, lots of Japanese construction companies made their way here to inspect the island. They wanted to build beach resorts and bigger highways, so they started buying up land and property and destroying the surrounding mountains. Many people, especially those up north in Nago City, refused to sell their land, preferring to protect the natural beauty of the area instead of watching it crumble away. Plus, we Okinawans were taught in school and at home that God [*kamisama*] exists in the mountains. We shouldn't anger him by disrupting his home. Well, as time went by, many people in Nago started to give in and began selling their land to construction companies or working construction and road-crew jobs to facilitate the development of the resorts. They must've been offered a lot of money by the mainland Japanese to do these things or they wouldn't have changed their minds. It's a shame that attendance at PTA [Parent-Teacher Association] meetings and village events dropped off as people were too busy making extra money at these side jobs to participate. This hurt human relations among the people in the area. The whole development scheme hurt the environment as well. After the mountains were cleared away, soil started flowing into the sea. Now every time it rains, the sea gets dirty.

In March 1974, Nakamura-san retired from her forty-year teaching career and took a position as vice-president of the Okinawa Women's Association.[14] *In her role as vice-president, she was deeply involved with the Ichi Feet Movement (Okinawa Historical Film Society), an organization designed to spread information about the Battle of Okinawa to people throughout the world. In June 1986, she retired from the Women's Association and joined the Ichi Feet Movement as secretary, a posi-*

tion she holds currently. Nakamura-san talked about her involvement with Ichi Feet, *and the organization's work in creating films about the war.*

Ichi Feet was created in 1983[15] to spread information about the Battle of Okinawa to people around the world. World War II, in particular the Battle of Okinawa, was so terrible that many of us on the island wanted to tell the world about it. Tens of thousands of Okinawans lost their lives and why? We were a peaceful nation for centuries before our island was sacrificed to save the mainland. It doesn't make sense. It's hard not to feel bitter about the suffering we had to endure.

The goal of *Ichi Feet* from the beginning was to purchase films and photos taken in Okinawa by American photographers during the war. Did you know there are thousands of feet of film from Okinawa and mainland Japan located in the National Archives in Washington, D.C.? We heard about these films from Okinawan exchange students who went to the States to study and from Japanese professors who had done research in Washington, D.C. Well, the members of *Ichi Feet* decided to purchase copies of some of these films and use them here to educate people about the war.

The *Ichi Feet* group was inspired by a similar group in Hiroshima, Japan, called the Ten Feet Movement. The people of Hiroshima had a fund-raising campaign to purchase footage from films taken by American photographers after the atomic bombing of Hiroshima in August 1945. They calculated they could purchase ten feet of footage for one thousand yen [approximately eight dollars],[16] and so campaigned on this slogan.

We decided to do the same thing here in Okinawa. We knew one foot of film from Washington cost around one hundred yen [approximately eighty cents], so we used "ichi feet" [one foot] as our slogan. Then we solicited donations throughout Okinawa to help pay for the cost of this footage. We figured everyone, even students, could afford to donate one hundred yen to help us out.

Ichi Feet's first film, *Okinawa sen: Mirai e no shōgen* [The Battle of Okinawa: Testimony for the Future] was completed in May 1986. That's when the group started showing it around the country for free. Telephone and mail requests from people asking us to show the film at their school or organization came pouring into the office. From the first time the documentary was shown, it received terrific reviews, and purchases of the video were overwhelming!

In 1988, the English version of the film was ready. We got requests for the film from groups in places as far away as South America[17] and the United States. We even ended up sending copies of the film to organizations in San

Francisco, New York, Los Angeles, and Honolulu before we visited those cities in 1988. You see, that year the United Nations held the Third Session of the United Nations Special Meeting on Disarmament in New York. Our *Ichi Feet* group attended as a nongovernmental organization (NGO). While we were in New York, we submitted a copy of the English version of the film to the UN. Then we traveled to cities on the West Coast to hold showings of the film there.

We had an interesting experience in Honolulu. There were lots of Japanese-American viewers, along with a fair number of people from other countries. At the end of the film, an elderly white woman approached me and, through the aid of an interpreter, said she'd come to the showing to oppose it. She had wondered why there was a "Jap movie" about the war playing. Then, as she watched the film, her feelings changed. "I was all choked up when I saw the suffering the common Okinawan people had to endure during the war. You should show this film all over the world," she recommended as tears streamed down her face.

We had another unusual experience when we showed the film to a group of elementary school children on Okinawa. When the tape was finished, a little boy in first grade asked me if the people in the movie were still living.

"Still living?" I asked, confused. "They died in the war, just like the film showed."

He looked bewildered. "You mean, it's not like the real movies where the people are killed on the screen but then they're OK when the movie's finished?"

I explained to him that this documentary portrayed what really happened to people; that the individuals on the screen weren't actors, but real human beings who had died in the war. "When you go home tonight ask your parents or your grandparents about the war and see what they tell you," I encouraged him.

The boy asked his grandfather that night if the war was as bad as what he'd seen on the screen that afternoon.

"No, it wasn't," his grandfather replied. "It was worse."

I heard about this from the boy's mother who called here the next day and told me what happened. She thanked me for creating the film and showing it to the students. She said her entire family was going to go and see the film together. That's what I wanted. I hoped different generations of people would watch together and then decide to talk about the war. I also hoped people would be inspired by the film to begin reading more and more about the Battle of Okinawa.

In 1995, *Ichi Feet* produced a second film called, *Document Okinawa* [Document: The Battle of Okinawa]. It was created in honor of the fi anniversary of the end of World War II. Like the first film, it was w ceived. We're even considering doing a third film about life in the reloc camps throughout Okinawa in the early postwar period. I think it's important to let people around the world know what happened here on the island. Most people know about the tragedies in Hiroshima and Nagasaki, but few people seem to be aware of the catastrophe that occurred on Okinawa. We need to spread information about the situation here on the island fifty years ago so that history doesn't repeat itself.

Nakamura-san concluded by discussing her feelings about the large American military presence on the island, and what sort of influence this foreign presence has had on Okinawans over the past half century.

I think the American Occupation has had both a positive and negative effect on Okinawa. Even though I'm against war and the existence of the bases here, that doesn't mean I'm against Americans as individuals. I think people often confuse the two and think that because some of us protest against the American presence, we're anti-American. That's not the case. I like it when the Americans, military or otherwise, show an interest in Okinawan customs and traditions. There are a lot of festivals and community events in Okinawa and everyone on the island is invited to participate in them. Plus, we're all human beings, aren't we? And, for the present time, we have to live in this small region together, so we should try to get along for the most part.

I guess there's a bit of inconsistency in everyone's feelings. Here I am saying I'm against the military presence on the island, but I'm happy when I see that Americans want to learn something about our culture. It's complicated, that's for sure. When I look at military personnel I think of them as human beings, just like anyone else. But then when I think about the types of things they do each day, and the sort of war drills they practice, it makes me angry.

Because of the American influence on the island, we Okinawans have been exposed to American arts, the English language, and different ways of living. Personally speaking, my outlook on life has become broader, and I've developed a more international way of looking at things. I learned a lot about a foreign culture without ever leaving Okinawa.

Those were the good effects of the American Occupation. Of course, the bad influence is the concentration of so many military bases on Okinawa. It bothers me that the men and women behind the steel fences use weapons and perform all sorts of war simulation exercises, especially considering

Okinawa's history of peace. I think this type of training can change people's behavior. For example, consider that rape case from three years ago.[18] The mother of one of the defendants refused to believe her son could commit such a heinous crime. She insisted he was a good boy, that he used to go to church every Sunday when he lived at home. I believe the woman when she says her son was a decent boy; I think it was the military that changed him, though. How could he *not* be affected by the drills they perform? They actually learn how to kill and hurt people. That's what I'm opposed to.

I blame both the American government and the Japanese government equally for the problems Okinawa is dealing with today. There needs to be more discussion about Okinawa when representatives from our two countries get together. If the American military were to leave the island, I think the Japanese government owes it to the Okinawans to help us out financially. A complete American withdrawal would undoubtedly hurt the economy here. But that shouldn't deter us from protesting against the removal of the bases. It isn't natural for a tiny island like ours to house 75 percent of the U.S. military bases in Japan. I don't think we need the bases at all. I mean, who wants to invade Okinawa? Many people say North Korea poses a threat in Asia. What do we have here that they might want, though? Okinawa isn't a rich place. And we aren't a threat militarily. I think if we're targeted now it's because, ironically, there's a foreign military presence here.

Okinawa is blessed geographically. It's a subtropical island surrounded by various Asian countries. What a chance for international exchange! In fact, when Okinawa was known as the Ryukyu Kingdom, it enjoyed diplomatic and trade relations with other countries such as Taiwan, China, the Philippines, all the way down to Java (Indonesia). That's why there's a heavy Asian influence in our music, art, and culture here. In fact, when I visited Indonesia and Malaysia, I went to a folk music recital and was surprised at how much the music resembled Okinawan music. I thought it *was* Okinawan music. I hope we can develop close relationships with these countries again like we had in the past.

At the same time we need to protect our own culture and have pride in things that are truly Okinawan. I think young people on the island are becoming more and more conscious of this. In fact, these days there's even an Okinawa *Hōgen Taikai* [an Okinawan dialect-speaking contest] on the island. And to think that in the prewar period our students were forbidden from using the dialect! It was all part of mainland Japan's policy of assimilation. Those students who were overheard speaking in dialect in the prewar period were forced to wear a sign around their necks labeling them as dialect speakers. The way to get rid of the sign was by getting another student to speak in dialect. Sort of like policing one another, huh?

We Okinawans have always been made to feel inferior by the Japanese. This has been going on since the Meiji era.[19] But nowadays I think young Okinawans especially are proud of their heritage; they have confidence in their ability to succeed, just like the mainland Japanese. Lots more young people these days are trying to get jobs here after they graduate from college. Back in the 1960s when Japan was experiencing its period of high economic growth, almost all of the young people on the island wanted to work in Tokyo. These days, though, more of them are staying here, or at least returning to Okinawa after a brief time on the mainland.

Nakamura-san rested her hands on the metal table in front of us and looked me in the eye.

You asked me once if I ever get tired of protesting, sick of standing up for what I truly believe in. Never. I'll always stick to my beliefs. If I were to quit now, that would mean I lost. I can't do that. I experienced one of life's greatest tragedies: war. Maybe that's hard for people who've never experienced such a horrendous thing to understand. But I never want something like that to happen again. So, for the sake of my children, my grandchildren, and my great-grandchildren, I'll continue in my attempt to educate people all over the world about the folly of war and the beauty of peace.

CHILDREN OF
THE OCCUPATION

4 : TATSUKO YAMADA

Watching Ryūbū, *or traditional Ryukyuan dance, is like turning the dial of a kaleidoscope. Images of lemon-yellow* bingata *(stencil-dyed fabric of Okinawa), grape-colored sashes, and cherry-red hats splashed with turquoise wave patterns, dance before the eyes, exciting the senses. As the performers twist and turn, their movements expose other bursts of color; a rotation of changing patterns. At last, the dancers group together, lifting their red-and-black rhythm blocks to forehead height before pulling their hands away from one another and unlinking, their separation unleashing a new brightly colored design.*

Ryūbū *is a visual art, one that symbolizes the beauty of the island and the richness of its culture. Over the years* Ryūbū *has had many functions. It was developed in the fifteenth century as a form of entertainment for visiting dignitaries from China. As the years passed and circumstances changed,* Ryūbū *evolved into an art form popular among commoners. Then, in the immediate postwar years, it played a significant role in bolstering the morale of the displaced islanders and in helping them regain their lost sense of self. Even today this classical dance is studied by many Okinawan men and women as a way of getting in touch with their past. The preservation of this performing art, many islanders claim, is the key to conserving Okinawa's heritage.*

Tatsuko Yamada *is a 57-year-old native Okinawan and one of the island's most well-known and respected instructors of* Ryūbū. *She is a sophisticated woman with a round face, high cheekbones, and black eyes that smile from behind large rose-colored glasses. She wears her hair pulled away from her face and wrapped tightly into a bun at the back of her head. The owner and operator of a* dōjō *for dance instruction in Futenma, the town in which she was raised, Yamada Sensei*[1] *teaches dance to all ages of people, from elementary school students to middle-aged women. She herself continues to practice classical dance faithfully with her instructor of thirty-seven years, Yoshiko Majikina. During my year on the island I had the pleasure of studying* Ryūbū *with Yamada Sensei.*

Our discussions took place at her dōjō. *The interior of the dance studio has beautiful sand-colored hardwood floors and a wall of large square windows. A rectangular mirror stretches across the entire length of one wall, while pictures and plaques crowd another. The shelf running along the back of the* dōjō *holds her trophies from dozens of dance recitals.*

During our conversations, Yamada Sensei discussed the role of performance art in the postwar period, and why the American occupiers were so interested in revitalizing traditional Okinawan dance in the aftermath of war. She also talked of her own family's involvement in the fine arts, and how the U.S. military supported their talents. The beneficiary of special treatment from the American occupiers in the early postwar period, Yamada Sensei holds fond memories of the Americans. Her impression of the mainland Japanese, though, is more critical. She recalls with disappointment the discrimination she experienced as an Okinawan in Tokyo during the 1960s and the frustration she felt over the unfair terms of reversion to Japan in 1972. These memories, along with her personal feelings regarding the effect of the U.S. military presence on the island, provide a fascinating look at life on Okinawa in the decades following the end of World War II.

I was just a young child during wartime, so I don't remember much about those days. The only thing I can recall is my mother and father's arguments. My mother used to mutter that Japan was going to lose the war, and my father used to holler back, "Japan is not going to be defeated!" I don't know if he really believed that or not, but that's what he used to shout at her.

I remember the immediate postwar years well. I was 5 years old when the fighting ended here on Okinawa. Following the Japanese surrender, my family was sent to a relocation camp in Ishikawa Village[2] for a year before we were permitted to move back to our hometown. We'd been living in Naha, the capital, before the war, but we didn't return there afterward. Instead we

CHILDREN OF THE OCCUPATION

moved to Futenma. That's because my father got a job with the U.S. military. He was an illustrator for the *Daily Okinawan*,[3] the first newspaper established by the Occupation forces. You see, the U.S. military had heard my father was a well-known artist and wanted to take advantage of his talents. So, they hired him to do drawings of life in Okinawa's prewar period as a way of teaching the American Occupation forces here something about Okinawa prior to the war. They wanted to know everything about the island from its customs and traditions, to its food and architecture. So my father made drawings to illustrate what life was like. His sketches were printed in the newspaper about once a week.

I don't think my father received a salary for his work, but he was compensated in other ways. For example, once a week a gigantic military truck rolled up to our house to deliver food. We used to get crates that looked like *bentō*[4] boxes filled with ice cream, canned goods, cookies, and milk. The milk and ice cream were in powdered form because we didn't have refrigerators at the time. We used to drink the ice cream like soup! We were lucky to get those sorts of things delivered right to our door since most people had to wait in long lines for their rations.

Because of my father's position as the newspaper artist, my family had a lot of contact with American GIs. When I was little, I remember the American soldiers coming around to take me for rides in their trucks or to play games with me outside. They spoiled me terribly! *She smiled.* Some of them even took me to church with them on Sundays. I'd sit there singing hymns right along with them. There was even a Catholic priest living nearby who used to take me with him on visits to people's homes. The best part of those outings was when he let me sip the grape wine used for the Eucharistic celebration. I'd never tasted anything so good in my life. In fact, maybe that's why I enjoy wine so much these days! Who knows?

Back in those early postwar years, it wasn't unusual for some Okinawans to have American foster families. My family had one — an army officer and his wife. They came around a lot when my mother was pregnant with my younger sister. That American wife was really eager to be my baby sister's godmother. In fact, she even asked my mother to name the baby after her. So when my little sister was born, my mother named her Dorothy. *She giggled.* Come to think of it, that couple liked to call all of us by American names. They referred to one of my younger brothers as Carl, and another as Henry. Over the years they were generous to my family. They always brought over boxes of diapers and clothes for Dorothy as she was growing up. Then, every year at Christmas time, they stopped by to deliver presents, as well as an enormous Christmas tree with all the trimmings.

We weren't the only people on the island who received special treatment from the Americans after the war. All people involved in the arts were treated well. One of the reasons why the Occupation forces were so generous toward performers here was because they wanted to make sure there were people to entertain and pacify the masses during all the commotion that followed the war. The Americans set up a place in Ishikawa where the entertainers gathered together then split into groups to form plays.[5] These troupes performed plays in different neighborhoods throughout the island as a way of cheering people up and giving them a little extra spirit to help them hang on. The entertainers didn't have *sanshin* [a three-stringed musical instrument] at the time, so they made simple ones from cans and then sewed costumes from parachutes and traveled around from neighborhood to neighborhood performing. Most of the actors at this time were professionals, people who'd been active in the theater before the war.

Each village, town, and city had a *rotengekijō* [open-air theater] where the actors performed. The types of performances they did varied. There were comedy routines as well as popular dance performances. Of course the *kagiyadefu*[6] was always performed since it's the main celebratory dance on the island. Naturally the Okinawans were excited to see these performances in the immediate postwar years since they reminded them of life before the war. But, as time passed, and conditions on the island returned to normal, more Okinawans were becoming interested in dances from the States and Europe. I guess that was because of the American influence here on the island. See, there was always some sort of dance performance or concert going on at one of the military bases here in the 1950s, so we Okinawans were well exposed to Western arts. We were fascinated by things like ballet and classical music because they were so different from what we were used to. Plus, I think we were suffering from a bit of an inferiority complex in those early postwar years. We wanted to be like Westerners. We thought maybe Western arts and dances were somehow "better" than Okinawan ones. After all, our customs and traditions and language had been disparaged for so long that maybe it was natural for us to try to adopt the culture of someone else. I don't know. *She shrugged.*

Anyhow, my father used to take my brothers and sisters and me to the military bases to listen to music, to look at paintings, and to watch dance performances. He thought being exposed to the fine arts was the first step in developing an appreciation for them. In fact, it was on one of the U.S. bases where I saw my first live ballet performance. I fell in love with ballet instantly. I remember sitting there wide-eyed while I watched the dancers on stage. Wow! What a sight that was! The beautiful costumes, the elegant music . . .

She closed her eyes and smiled in recollection. At that moment I knew without a doubt I wanted to become a ballerina.

I begged my father to let me take lessons. Unfortunately, he didn't have the money at the time. So I had to satisfy myself by peeking in the window of the dance studio in my neighborhood and watching the other girls perform. I'd memorize the steps, and then when I got back home, I'd practice them over and over again. By the time I reached junior high school, my father was finally able to afford lessons for me. I was thrilled!

I used to go to Naha, the capital, for my lessons. I practiced there three times a week with a Japanese woman who'd studied ballet in the States. I remember I used to wear a T-shirt and tights to practice. We couldn't afford toe shoes, so I borrowed them from a friend. At the time of the recital, though, my father managed to buy me a pair. Well, those shoes didn't get much use because I only participated in one recital. When my father saw my performance, he suggested I try another type of dance. He said my body shape didn't fit well with ballet. "Ballet wasn't made for Japanese; it was made for Westerners," I remember him saying. "And you'll never be a Westerner," he added. So I guess my career as a ballerina was fairly short-lived: just two years.

I wasn't interested in Okinawan dance at the time, but that's what I started studying next. My father thought classical Okinawan dance would help me in the future. He was convinced that learning *Ryūbū* would open up opportunities for me to travel around the world someday. He was right. Never in my wildest dreams did I imagine I'd get to perform in so many foreign countries. I've been lucky.

It's funny, but I hated *Ryūbū* from the very first lesson. The slow rhythm of the music just didn't appeal to me. I'd been listening to Western classical music for years as a child, so that was the rhythm I was used to. Even though I didn't like *Ryūbū,* I preferred to dance than to sit around at home or study, so I stuck with it. Then, one year after I began, we had a recital, and I won first place. That raised my spirits and gave me the confidence to continue.

Back in those days the dance instructors here were strict. And my teacher, Yoshiko Majikina, was probably one of the toughest. She used to make us practice for two hours everyday. A big part of our practice was learning how to walk correctly. You see, there's a special way to move your feet when performing *Ryūbū*. You have to put your heels in a certain position. *She demonstrated the movement.* It was hard to learn how to walk like this, especially when you have to bend slightly at the knees as if sitting down and then tilt the body forward at an angle. It's sort of like shaping your body into the form of the hiragana symbol *ku*.[7] Then, of course, we had to pay attention to our posture. I didn't have many problems with my posture because I'd taken ballet lessons.

There were about one hundred people in my *Ryūbū* class at the time. Everyone from elementary school students to older women. We didn't have *juku*[8] back then, and not many people could afford pianos, so there was nothing else to do but dance.

My parents never forced my brothers and sisters and me to study an art, even though they themselves were artists. Like I said, my father was a painter and sculptor, and my mother was a classical dancer. In fact, they met for the first time when my mother was on stage performing. She was from a poor household and had been sold by her parents when she was just 7 years old to a family who ran a Japanese restaurant. Her parents reasoned that she'd never go hungry if she lived with a family who owned a restaurant. So, my mother baby-sat for the children of that family while the parents worked. My mother was a real beauty, even at such a young age. And she had a talent for dance. That was evident the moment she started studying with a famous dance instructor on the island named Seigi Tamagusuku. She performed for the first time when she was 14 years old and was a real wonder, a natural dancer.

Well, my father came into the restaurant where my mother was performing one evening and fell in love with her at first sight. My mother was 18 years old at the time, and my father was 38. They got married shortly after they met. Once they were married, my father wouldn't let her continue dancing. There were a couple reasons for that. First, he was a bit of a *teishu kanpaku* [domineering husband]. He didn't want my mother leaving the house. "A wife should be at home with the kids," he used to say, wagging his finger. I don't think this bothered my mother too much; after all, she had seven kids to take care of, so she had plenty to keep her busy at home. Second, my father firmly believed that dance instruction was a profession for the lower class. That might seem strange because we generally think the arts are something for the rich, but rich people are usually the ones who watch dance performances and plays and listen to orchestras; they aren't the ones who perform.

Even though my mother had been doing classical dance in the prewar period, women weren't allowed to dance at all in those days. She was an exception because she was one of those women who performed in special restaurants catering to men. In general, though, women weren't permitted to perform in public.[9] It wasn't until the postwar period that women began performing dance regularly. A lot of them started teaching dance as a way of making a living. See, most of the male classical dance instructors were busy in the postwar period building military bases and roads throughout the island. That's when women had to take over as dance instructors to keep *Ryūbū* alive.

Not only did *Ryūbū* stay alive; it prospered magnificently. Especially around the end of the 1950s and beginning of the 1960s. It was the Americans on the island who recognized the value and beauty of Ryukyuan dance and expressed an interest in fostering its continuation. I guess they were intrigued by Okinawa's history and culture, which is reflected in the dance. Well, once the Americans showed an interest in Ryukyuan dance, the Okinawans, too, started to look again at their traditional arts and realize the beauty inherent in them.

These days, *Ryūbū* is more popular than Western dance in Okinawa. All of the dances on the island, from *Ryūbū* to *Eisa*[10] to folk dances, represent Okinawa and symbolize our pride and identity, but *Ryūbū's* probably the dance form people know best. That's because the performers wear colorful *bingata* and move to the music of the *sanshin*, music that's traditionally Okinawan. Just looking at *Ryūbū* you can tell instantly what it's all about. Aesthetically speaking, it *is* Okinawa.

Yamada Sensei's cellular phone rang, and she pulled it from her purse to answer it. After several moments she resumed our conversation, this time focusing on her impression of relations between Okinawans and mainland Japanese throughout the years.

In 1962, I went away to college on the mainland. I attended Keio University in Tokyo where I studied Japanese literature. My parents didn't force me to go to college or anything. They told my brothers and sisters and me that we should do whatever we wanted to do in life. If that involved going to college, then, OK, go to college. If not, then we should find something else to do. They just wanted us to be happy.

It was difficult for an Okinawan to be on the mainland in those years. I remember feeling a lot of discrimination from the Japanese up there. For example, some people refused to speak with me when they heard I was from Okinawa. One girl even asked me not to sit with her and her friends at lunch in the cafeteria. Back then Okinawa had a reputation as a place where the men drank all the time; a wild, savage, and dirty place. There were even bars and restaurants on the mainland that put signs out front saying, "Okinawans Prohibited." That was because Okinawan people were notorious for drinking a lot and then starting fights.

These days Okinawa isn't as bad as it used to be, but there are still drunks who sleep in the streets here. They just pee wherever they feel like it. Probably smells out there in front of my house right now. My mother used to stand outside with her arms planted across her chest and stare the drunks down while they urinated in front of our gate. She never said anything to them; just gave them a good hard stare. *Yamada Sensei demonstrated the look before erupting into laughter.*

The mainland Japanese still don't understand much about us Okinawans. They're always asking things like, "Do Okinawans living in rural areas of the island wear shoes?" and "Can everyone on Okinawa speak standard Japanese?" One month ago when I went to Sendai[11] on the mainland to perform classical Okinawan dance, a few people there admitted they never knew classical dance even existed on Okinawa. "We thought you danced around naked!" they confessed. "You know, like the people in Papua New Guinea and all." So, discrimination toward Okinawans hasn't completely disappeared. But I have to admit, there isn't as much discrimination here as there is in the United States.

Five years ago I went to North Carolina with a group of dancers to perform *Ryūbu*. We danced at a place located about two hours from a big military base in that state. There are a lot of middle-aged Okinawan women living near the base because they're married to American men in the military. They met here on the island in the days before reversion when there were lots of American men stationed on Okinawa. I talked with these women after our performance, and they confessed how miserable they were living in the States. Apparently they had trouble fitting in with Americans because they were foreign wives brought over from Asia.

These women couldn't run away because they didn't have any money or a place to go. When they met their American husbands on Okinawa, these men were rich. But you have to remember that that was compared to Okinawan society, which was really poor. These women had no idea that once they married American men and moved to the States they'd be in a lower social class than they were here. But that's what happened. These men had turned out to be not as well off in the States as they were in Okinawa, and they couldn't give the women the lifestyle they'd been dreaming of. Consequently, a lot of them were disillusioned after being in the States for a while.

I think that's why so many of them were moved by our dance performance; they were longing for home, and simply hearing the slow *sanshin* music and seeing our colorful costumes made them even more nostalgic for the island. Almost all of them were crying after the performance.

Discrimination against Okinawans is nothing new; it's been going on for a long, long time. I remember my father telling me about the hardships he had as a young man on the mainland in the early part of this century. My father went to Tokyo for the first time when he was 15 years old. When he was a child in Yaeyama,[12] he made a boat out of bamboo to play with in the river.

He put a *senkō* [incense stick] in the top and lit it, watching the smoke circles in the air. It was a fabulous piece of work. A carpenter in the saw it and asked who'd made the creation. People told him that my made it. He said my father had tremendous talent and should be in Tokyo, not Yaeyama. So shortly thereafter, he was apprenticed to a sculptor on the mainland, a man by the last name of Yamada. Eventually he was adopted by Mr. Yamada and changed his last name from "Tokashiki" to "Yamada." Then my father married the daughter of a painter up there on the mainland, and they had four kids together. Unfortunately that woman refused to move to Okinawa. She'd been here once before and swore she wouldn't come back. "Too poor, too dirty," she complained. So my father returned alone. Shortly after his return, he discovered my mother dancing in that restaurant and married her.

Anyhow, back in the days when he was in Tokyo, there was a sculpture contest in which one artist from each of Japan's forty-seven prefectures was solicited to create a piece of art. My father was the representative from Okinawa. He was 18 years old at the time. Well, each of the participants had to sculpt something from wood, and then a council of sculptors chose the best creation. That piece was then purchased by the Emperor and Empress of Japan. My father won first place, but can you imagine what happened? The council decided that first prize couldn't go to an Okinawan, so they picked someone else for the grand prize and gave my father second place. Okinawans were really discriminated against by the mainlanders in those prewar years. They thought we were backward and dirty, incompetent island people.

Even after the war they continued to think this way. But despite their feelings of superiority toward us, we Okinawans still wanted to reunite with the mainland. People here were tired of the American Occupation and felt it was only natural that Okinawa be recognized as a part of Japan again. We used to say Okinawa was like a child being reunited with its parent: Japan. I remember everyone here at the time waving *Hinomaru* [Japanese flags] in support of reunion with the motherland. In fact, I even recall a bunch of Okinawans gathering together at *Hedomisaki* [Hedo Point] — the spot on the island that's closest to the mainland geographically — where they lit torches and waved *Hinomaru* in the direction of the mainland as a sign of support for reversion.

Another way we Okinawans at the time showed our enthusiasm toward reuniting with mainland Japan was by referring to ourselves as "Japanese," not "Okinawans." Nowadays you'll rarely hear an Okinawan call himself a Japanese. We usually refer to ourselves as "*uchinanchu.*" That's Okinawan dialect for "a person from Okinawa."

Unfortunately, after reversion in 1972, nothing changed on the island. We thought the U.S. military bases would disappear from Okinawa and conditions here would become equal to those on the mainland. Well, we were wrong. The Japanese government didn't do a thing for us. The only difference was that we no longer needed a passport to travel to the mainland. Needless to say, we Okinawans were disappointed. It was like we'd been betrayed by the Japanese. Suddenly all of those *Hinomaru* disappeared from the island. No one even put the flag out on New Year's Day like they were accustomed to doing in the pre-reversion days. Yes, *she nodded slowly,* we Okinawans felt double-crossed by mainland Japan.

During the early years of the American Occupation, Yamada Sensei and her family enjoyed a close relationship with members of the U.S. military, mainly because of her father's job as an artist. As time passed, and economic conditions on the island improved, her family's direct contact with the American military lessened. However, the Yamadas continued to come in contact with GIs and their dependents on the streets of Futenma, an area of Ginowan City close to Futenma Marine Air Station where more than three thousand American military personnel are stationed. She shared with me her feelings about the American presence on the island, and how she believes she has been affected by it over the years.

Looking back over the past fifty years since the end of the war, I don't think I've been greatly affected by the American presence here on the island. I sort of feel like a third party, a spectator here sometimes. In other words, I didn't have land confiscated, and I didn't suffer any particular damage — physical or mental — from the war. Perhaps that's different from how a lot of people on the island perceive their own situation, but it's an accurate description of how I feel personally.

Having said that, I guess I should add that my family's relationship with the U.S. military in the immediate postwar years was an unusual one. Because of my father's position as the newspaper artist, we received all sorts of special treatment from the Americans. For instance, we always had plenty of food and a nice place to live. When I look back on my life as a child here, my memories are pleasant ones. So, I probably *was* affected by the American presence, but in a positive way, not a negative way.

Whenever we Okinawans are asked about the influence of the Americans here, we can't help but think of the bases. I'm reminded of the bases every day because I live close to Futenma Marine Air Station. There are always helicopters and planes flying over the *dōjō* here, so naturally it can get noisy. Sometimes even the glass in the windows shakes. I think I've gotten used to the noise, though, over the years. It doesn't bother me all that much anymore.

As far as the American military personnel themselves, of course I see them on the streets all the time, but the numbers are nothing compared to what they were in the years before reversion. At that time, the area in front of the *dōjō* was lined with A-sign[13] bars and restaurants, so there were always groups of Americans walking around. Only the GIs, or Okinawans affiliated with the bases, could afford to eat out in those days, so if a restaurant didn't have an A-sign, it probably didn't stay in business for long. All the A-sign establishments have disappeared, but we still see Americans on the streets out front since the Marine base is just behind the fence. *She pointed out the dōjō window in the direction of the base.*

The whole issue of the U.S. bases here is a political problem. Take a look at that situation in Nago City up north where they're talking about building a heliport. In the future that's going to be a mess. Right now the people of Nago may benefit financially from the construction of the heliport, which is why they can't afford to think about the future. But they should. That whole situation is just another example of how the Japanese government is sacrificing Okinawa for the sake of the mainland. The heliport issue is something that's being handled solely between the governments of the United States and Japan. It's like Okinawa doesn't even have a say in what's happening. That's not fair considering the heliport's going to be located right here in our prefecture.

The Japanese government doesn't do much to make Okinawa a more prosperous place. Before the war Okinawa was a poor island. People running around barefoot in old kimono and all. The only real industries here were pineapple and sweet potato production. And you can't maintain a healthy economy on just that. So, after the war we became dependent on the bases. That's what kept our unemployment rate so low. Then the tourist industry started to flourish about fourteen or fifteen years ago. But tourism is still only half-developed on Okinawa. If we truly want to be a tourist island, the land from the bases needs to be returned so we can use it in other ways. Plus, the Japanese government is obligated to pump more money into the economy here to get the tourist industry functioning properly.

I guess the non-existence of the bases is the ideal situation for Okinawa, but if the Japanese government isn't going to help us out, then we need the bases to stay alive economically. If the government decides to support us, it can capitalize on the fact that Okinawa is a coral island. After all, there isn't any coral on the mainland; we have something they don't have. So, let's use that to our advantage. I guess what it comes down to is that a lot of problems here need to be addressed by the Japanese government and shouldn't be blamed entirely on the bases. People forget that the military bases have made a great contribution to the Okinawan economy over the years. The fact that the bases were here enabled us Okinawans to eat.

Despite the problems that exist on the island, I never think of living anywhere but Okinawa. It's not too hot here, or too cold. Well, the summer *does* get hot, but there's a nice breeze, so it doesn't feel too bad. There are lots of places in the world where I can travel, but Okinawa, in my opinion, is the only place to live!

5 : MASAYO HIRATA

The office of International Social Assistance Okinawa, Inc. (ISAO), is hidden in a crowded residential area behind Jiro Bakery in Kiyuna, not far from Futenma Marine Air Station. Riding my bicycle along Route 330 in search of ISAO, I found myself stopping frequently to absorb the sights in the area. My senses were overwhelmed by strings of electric wires suspended precariously over flimsy wooden shops, stores overflowing with chunky American-style furniture, and English language signs advertising places such as House of 66 Cents and American Variety Shop. Bright red Coca-Cola signs and towheaded American dolls peeked out from window displays where cardboard signs promising the lowest prices in town lured both Okinawan and American shoppers inside.

I pulled off the main road, thankful for some respite from the relentless traffic. Following a narrow side street northward, I finally recognized the sign for ISAO. I locked up my bike then pulled open the metal door of the office and glanced around the interior. The place was bare, a sparsely furnished office with moss-colored tiled floors and sea-green walls. A few leather armchairs and a low marble-topped coffee table decorated the waiting area. Under the table lay several children's books, a toy xylophone, and a wooden puzzle with a missing piece.

I rang the tiny silver bell on the reception desk and waited for someone to arrive. Within seconds, footsteps sounded hollowly across the tiled floor. I looked around to see Masayo Hirata, a stylish 58-year-old woman with curly gray hair and an illuminating smile, heading toward me hurriedly.

"Good morning!" she welcomed me. "I'm glad you found the place OK. As you can see I'm the only one here," she said, stretching out her hand and spanning the office. Then she directed me to one of the meeting rooms located down the hall.

"I'll sit here near the door in case the phone rings," she said as she took a seat on the tawny-colored sofa facing me. "We had to cut back on staff here since we're closing our doors in March 1998. I guess there just isn't as much need for this organization now as there was in the past," she said. Then she handed me some literature regarding ISAO and its functions.

International Social Assistance Okinawa, Inc., was established in 1958 by International Social Services America. It was originally designed as an adoption agency dedicated to finding American families for thousands of biracial children on the island. These days the center's functions are varied. ISAO focuses on assisting biracial children and their parents with professional counseling, education, and administrative support, as well as providing marriage counseling services for Okinawan women and their American husbands. It is the only social welfare center of its kind on the island. Masayo Hirata has worked at ISAO as a social worker for thirty years. Her education in social work in the United States and her marriage to an American serviceman prepared her for many of the problems that her clients face, such as questions regarding child support payments, legal issues related to international marriages and adoptions, and problems in interpreting behavior from a partner of a different culture.

Hirata-san and I generally met at her office in the late morning hours. During our interview sessions she talked about her life on Okinawa during the postwar period, from her role as a student activist in the 1960s to her career as a social worker over the past three decades. She also discussed what it was like to be married to an American and the issues that cross-cultural couples and their biracial children face in Okinawan society today. Hirata-san's reminiscences provide insight into social conditions on Okinawa during the past four decades and the effect the U.S. military presence has had on the local populace, especially women, over the years.

I used to be married to an American. We wed in 1966. My husband was in the military for a few years until he decided to take a job in insurance sales here on the island. He didn't speak much Japanese at the time, but he always made an effort to study it.

We didn't have a lot in common now that I look back on things. I think it was the initial excitement of having an American suitor that appealed to me. You see, I wasn't used to men approaching me. Okinawan men are reluctant to approach a woman if they think they don't have a chance of marrying her. I don't know about the States, but here on the island a man considers a woman's social class before asking her out on a date. Then usually two people of the same social standing marry one another. Well, a lot of men were apprehensive about asking me out, probably because they knew I'd been to a good college on the mainland and was planning to attend graduate school in the States. Not many people back then had the opportunity to do those sorts of things.

When this American man showed an interest in me, I was really excited. His name was Mike, and I met him before I went to the States for graduate school. I did my undergraduate work at Waseda University in Tokyo, and then returned to Okinawa and was awarded a scholarship from the U.S. Army to do my graduate work in the States. Originally I entered Waseda University to study Japanese literature. I ended up changing my major to English literature, though, after consulting with my parents and professors. They seemed to agree that English was going to be an important language in Okinawa's future. They were right. It didn't matter so much to me what I majored in; my main concern at the time was just getting to Tokyo where the best schools were.

I was a student at Waseda University from 1958 to 1962. What a time that was! All university students there were involved in the ANPO[1] demonstrations [to protest the Security Treaty between Japan and the United States]. It was almost as if we had no choice. "This isn't the time for studying; get out there and do something!" the main student activists urged us. Personally I was demonstrating against the Security Treaty because of the situation in Okinawa. See, the treaty was responsible for the proliferation of military bases here on the island. I don't think most of the activists were thinking about Okinawa in particular while they were demonstrating, though; they were simply against war and the existence of a security pact between Japan and the United States. They thought it would lead Japan into another war. Things in Vietnam were heating up at the time, and the United States was using its bases on mainland Japan and in Okinawa as a starting point for missions into Vietnam. People were worried that Japan would become implicated in another war just after it had begun to bounce back economically and psychologically from the devastation of fifteen years earlier.

There were two ANPO demonstrations. The first occurred in 1960, and the second one a decade later in 1970. I was involved in the first generation of ANPO demonstrations when I was a junior in college. It was a pure generation, an idealistic one. We skipped classes at the time because of all the commotion and activity. Groups of students even blocked the doorways to the school buildings to prevent anyone from going in. Not even the professors were around.

Some student activists were more radical than others. I wasn't one of them; I was more of a follower than a leader. The really vocal students were the ones who were arrested. They led us in chanting things like "Yankee, go home!" at our demonstrations. I felt funny about repeating those words because it seemed like I was attacking someone personally. And I wasn't doing that. Like a lot of people, I thought the things President Eisenhower and Prime Minister Ikeda were doing — mainly supporting the Security Treaty — were wrong. But I didn't think they were intrinsically bad people. Our demonstrations at the time were so heated they prevented President Eisenhower from coming to the mainland. He was on a tour of Asia at the time and was scheduled to make a stop in Tokyo, but the demonstrations kept him away. The student leaders saw that as a great success.[2]

I can still remember what I wore when I demonstrated. It's funny the things we remember, isn't it? I can't recall what I wore two days ago, but I know exactly what I had on when I protested in front of the Diet Building[3] in Tokyo in 1960. I was wearing a skirt with two huge pockets, one on each side. In each pocket I had things like tissues and a handkerchief and a little bit of money. Just enough money to get home on the train. I didn't carry a bag or purse with me since it'd just get in the way as I locked arms with the others and moved through the streets.

I remember securing my pockets shut with two big safety pins. Then I tied my hair back in two ponytails to keep it from getting in my face. Of course, I didn't carry any identification on me just in case I was caught or arrested. My parents were worried about this. They thought if the government or police knew I was involved in demonstrations it'd jeopardize my chances at finding a job once I returned to Okinawa. They were also worried that I was going to get my passport confiscated. At that time we Okinawans had to have a passport to travel from Okinawa to the mainland.

One of the funniest things about these demonstrations in Tokyo were the songs we sang. *She buried her face in her hands in embarrassment.* When I think back to this, it makes me laugh. We had to sing all sorts of songs from the Russian Revolution and the French Revolution. You know, songs that were supposed to inspire in us the spirit of the working man. I always thought they were just plain old demonstration songs. We used to do the Russian ones in Japanese, and the French ones in French. *She sang a few bars of a French revolutionary song for me.* I remember the words to that one well. Maybe that's because I studied French at Waseda.

It wasn't until years later when I was watching a documentary about the ANPO demonstrations on TV that I realized those songs were ones inspired by foreign revolutions. My God, I thought, *that's* what we were singing? I was shocked.

When I returned to Okinawa from Tokyo, I went to work at the culture center in the USO [United Service Organization] on Kadena Air Base. That was in 1963. I know, it may seem contradictory to campaign against the bases and then to take a job on one. Maybe I was motivated by selfish reasons. You see, at the time I was thinking about going to the States to study, and I knew I needed to improve my English. I was an English literature major at Waseda, but I wasn't able to use vocabulary from Shakespeare or the Canterbury Tales in daily American conversation! Waseda is like that; we were taught the classics, but very little about how to communicate in daily life. So I had to learn that on base. I stayed at that job for about two years. Most of the other girls who were working there with me were on the same time schedule. All of us wanted to improve our English enough to pass the test offered by the U.S. Army scholarship committee to study in America.

This is difficult to explain, but I guess I'd developed a bit of an elitist attitude while attending university on the mainland. I knew I was one of a handful of students in the country who was lucky enough to get a university education. I capitalized on that elite role, wearing pins on my clothing identifying myself as a Waseda student. Actually, all university students at the time did those sorts of things. The men even walked around wearing special caps that looked like policemen's hats with a square top and a visor in the front. One glance at those caps and you knew the guys were Waseda students. At the time it was popular among the guys to wear the caps their fathers or grandfathers had worn when they were at Waseda years before. New-looking caps weren't fashionable at all. That's why the guys who didn't have old caps bought stiff new ones and took them to a hatter who made them look old. He usually smeared raw egg on the caps, or put them through the washing machine or something to make them look used. *She laughed.*

The elitist attitude I developed in Tokyo stayed with me when I returned to Okinawa from the mainland. While I was working at the USO, I thought I was different from everybody else. I thought because I was a college graduate I shouldn't have to talk with the high school dropouts who hung around the USO. I tried to keep some distance between them and me, to be professional and serious. What I didn't realize for a long time was that to the Americans I was nothing but an ordinary young girl. To them my achievements meant nothing. They didn't care if I had good grades or went to a top university. And they were bold! They didn't hesitate to approach me, or stammer around trying to find the right words to say. They generally just came right up and tried to engage me in conversation. The longer I worked at the USO the more I understood I wasn't so different from anyone else. It was a painful realization. But I think it was a good lesson for me.

At the USO I worked as a program staff person. I was responsible for informing servicemen about social happenings occurring on and around the base, things like Ryukyuan dance recitals, karate exhibitions, and other events like that. We published literature about these special performances and then distributed it. I remember I used to ask one of the guys there to proofread the articles I wrote in English. This was Mike, the man I eventually married. I used to see him around the USO a lot because he used the library and study rooms there almost every day. He was always doing Japanese homework. He used to come around and question me about Japanese words. "What's this? What's that?" he'd ask.

Then one night at ten o'clock when I left work and went outside to wait for the bus, Mike walked along with me. Well, the bus never showed up. That's when he suggested giving me a ride home. I took him up on his offer. After all, it sure beat that slow bus ride all the way to Naha. I think he and I went out for coffee, too, that evening. I mean, it would've been rude not to have a drink with him after he drove me all that way.

Shortly afterward, I was awarded one of those U.S. Army scholarships to study in the States. I decided I wanted to pursue a master's degree in social work. I think my involvement in the ANPO demonstrations and my work on base inspired in me a desire to be with the common people, not separated from them. My parents weren't opposed to my decision to go to the States despite the complicated feelings many Okinawans had at that time [1965] toward the U.S. military presence here. My family wasn't rich, so my parents were grateful I was going to have the chance to receive further education abroad at no cost.

There were about forty Okinawans selected to study in the States. Twenty were sent to Hawaii, and the rest of us to various locations throughout mainland America. Well, I got sent to Buffalo, New York. Now how is an Okinawan supposed to survive a Buffalo winter? When I came back to Okinawa my hair was already gray! The same color it is now. *She twisted her index finger through a lock of silver hair.*

I didn't have a driver's license in the States. In fact, I don't have one here either. My husband used to tease me that I never got one because I liked being chauffeured around. When I was doing my social work training at a local hospital in Buffalo, I had to wait out in the cold for a friend to pick me up. I used to dread standing out there on the street corner all alone in the freezing cold. I kept thinking to myself, "This isn't the way humans should have to live." So, I left school just shy of a year and returned to Okinawa. I'd originally planned on staying in Buffalo for two years to complete the master's program, but the cold climate was too much for me. Did you know that it snows from October till April up there in Buffalo?

I guess there was another reason why I decided to leave New York. My friend, Mike, the one I met in Okinawa before I left for the States, got discharged from the air force and went home to Long Island, New York. We met up there and spent a lot of time together while I was a graduate student. I remember taking the Greyhound [bus] to see him at his home. And once we even traveled together to Niagara Falls. Then during the Easter holidays that year I visited him at his parents' home where he really pulled a surprise on me. He proposed to me right in front of everyone! Had the engagement ring and everything. You see, he'd spoken with my roommate beforehand to find out my ring size. I'll admit, I was genuinely surprised when he asked me to marry him. We'd never talked seriously about marriage. I cared for him a lot, but I don't know if I was all that eager to get married at the time. Maybe if the two of us had discussed it beforehand I would've felt more comfortable with the situation. But it was all so sudden. So there we were in front of his parents who were anxiously awaiting my response. How could I say no?

It's funny, but in America people think it's natural to get married simply because they love one another. We don't necessarily think that way here in Japan. More than a question of liking someone or disliking someone, marriage in Japan concerns the future. The man and woman discuss what sort of future they might have together, where they intend to live, and things like that. They look at the whole concept of marriage in a practical way. Then, after taking all of these issues into consideration, the two people might not end up getting married, even though they may love one another deeply. I think Americans find this difficult to understand. But for us Japanese, it's normal.

Anyhow, after accepting Mike's proposal, I had to start thinking about returning to Okinawa and preparing for the wedding. Mike had already decided to take a job in insurance sales on Okinawa. Back in the 1960s there were lots of American companies and organizations on the island, so it wasn't too hard for U.S. civilians to find work here. The first thing I did before following

Mike back to Okinawa was write a letter to my parents explaining the situation and telling them I was on my way back home.

They didn't appreciate the news. Actually, they were furious. When I got back home, not a word was spoken about this impending marriage. It was as if they refused to acknowledge it altogether. In the past, parents were strict about their daughters marrying American servicemen. These days they are, too, but not as much as in the past. It's not like all of us were marrying Americans at the time because we were dissatisfied with Okinawan men or anything. In fact, there were lots of Okinawan women who would've rather married Okinawan men since they know about the culture and customs of the island. It's nice to have someone who can manage things on religious holidays and all. Plus, some parents of girls here felt that their daughters should marry their own kind. Why go looking for an American when there are plenty of Okinawan men around? My parents never told me not to marry an American. They weren't prejudiced or anything. But they always thought if I married an American I would've married a doctor or a director of USCAR[4] or a general or someone, not just a regular guy in the service. If I hadn't married an American, I guess I probably would've married someone like a doctor. And then I would've spent the rest of my life arranging flowers and making tea. I'm glad things didn't turn out that way. I don't like that kind of lifestyle.

Since my parents weren't thrilled about my wedding, I made the preparations alone. I chose the church, then went to the market in Naha to buy a few meters of white organdy fabric to put over my head like a veil on my wedding day. I wasn't planning on wearing a wedding dress for the occasion, but rather a colorful kimono, the kind with long sleeves. When I finished all of my preparations, I told my parents when and where the wedding would take place. I had no idea if they were intending to show up or not, but I let them know the details anyhow.

My mother ended up calling some relatives and telling them the whole story. Everyone was shocked to hear about my wedding plans. I'll never forget their long faces as they sat there in our living room the day before the wedding. I'd been out running errands, and when I returned, the atmosphere in the living room was funereal! Honestly, I thought I'd just barged in on a wake or something. Everyone was so silent. I think they still couldn't get over the shock that I was marrying an American.

Our wedding was an informal affair. We got married in a church by an American priest since my husband was Catholic. Then we had a reception at Tokyu Hotel in Shuri afterward. My parents showed up at the wedding, along with some relatives and a few of our good friends from work. None of my husband's family came over from America, though. I didn't expect them to. I'd already met them when I was in the States.

Once we were married, my husband and I settled down here on Okinawa. Then he started his job in insurance sales. It was 1966. He did good business for a while because of his connections on base. Mike was one of those people everybody knew and admired.

Because he was a salesman, my husband had to develop and maintain a good rapport with people. That's why we were always going to some sort of party at the Chamber of Commerce or at one of the clubs on base. I really hated those social functions. Mike was forever introducing me to people whose names I couldn't remember. Once when we were out somewhere, he ran into someone he knew, and when I asked him later who that man was, he got angry and said, "Don't you remember? He's Colonel so-and-so. I introduced you to him last week!" Well, I don't have any interest in the military or their ranks, and it didn't mean much to me if he was a corporal, a sergeant, or a general.

When I accompanied my husband to certain social events, some Americans were hesitant to approach me because I'm Okinawan. I guess they figured I wouldn't be able to communicate with them. "Oh, you speak English well!" they'd say surprisingly after being introduced. After that, they'd ask me questions about the weather or some equally boring subject because they didn't know what else to say. "Have you been to the States? Really? For how long? Isn't that nice?" they'd comment. I couldn't wait to leave those parties! All the wives ever seemed to talk about was their bowling outings or their picnics. There's nothing wrong with that sort of conversation, but it just didn't suit me. Perhaps it was a cultural difference. I don't know.

I guess I was happiest when I met with a group of women whom I had attended school with in the past to chat casually and discuss contemporary issues. My husband never reacted well when I told him I was going to meet with the ladies. He used to erupt, "Oh, go ahead and talk with all your Ph.D. friends!" I tried to take him along with me on occasion, but he couldn't understand the conversation, and I ended up interpreting the whole time.

I didn't mind explaining things to him sometimes, but if I had to do it on every occasion it got tiring. I was always so mentally exhausted from interpreting. And, you know, sometimes I just wanted to be alone. It would've been nice on occasion to go somewhere like to a movie or out to eat by myself. In Japan that's not unusual. But in America it's strange for a person, especially a married person, to do that. At least my former husband said so. "People will think we're having marital problems," he used to say, and then insist on going out together. I felt so stifled.

If I managed to go out alone, I usually did things that didn't cost a lot of money, like looking at paintings at an art museum or listening to a lecture. We didn't have too much money back then because my husband worked on commission. And even though he could drive through the gates of the military bases easily, he didn't have base privileges since he was no longer with the air force. So we couldn't shop at the PX or commissary where things are cheap. We were strapped for cash most of the time. In fact, I remember we didn't have the money to purchase meat since it was so expensive. Honestly, I can't recall ever buying it. I made a lot of dishes with tofu. Thankfully our two sons liked it. [Hirata-san had one son a year after she married and another 12 years later.]

Gradually my husband and I started to drift apart. We just stopped doing things together. He went to the functions he needed to go to, and I went to places I wanted to go to. And even though I said I'd never divorce, I did. In our life together it was like I was here, *she said making a circle with the index finger and thumb of her right hand*, and he was here, *she continued, intertwining that loop with the same fingers of her left hand*, and our kids were in the middle.

Maybe things would've been easier for us had we lived in America. I don't know. Personally I was willing to go anywhere. But my husband wanted to be here on Okinawa. In fact, even though we divorced, he's still here on the island and lives nearby. I don't think it would've worked out had he gone back to the States. His parents died a long time ago, and his younger sister got married and moved away. Plus, he doesn't have a house or anything in the States. What's left for him there? All of his friends are here in Okinawa.

I don't know what things are like now, but twenty years or so ago, Americans were like big fish in a little pond here. I think he liked that. Back home he might've been just a small fish in a big ocean. I think he had more business chances here, too. Plus, he could rub elbows with generals and other high military officials at parties on base. He was psychologically satisfied here. The military was his reference group, the anchor that added stability to his life. I was against this. I didn't like feeling as if I was on the fringe of this type of society, caught in the middle between the local community and the base community. Unfortunately my kids were in this position. That confuses a child and his identity.

The issue of identity is a complicated one here in Okinawa. It's especially difficult for biracial children. See, there are lots of kids on the island with Okinawan mothers and American fathers. One of the biggest issues these children face concerns which group they're more a part of, the Okinawans or the

Americans. Sometimes the child is accepted by neither. And if the child has an American name like Mike or Bob, but a face indicating parents of two different races, that's another source of confusion for people and the genesis of other sorts of prejudice. Those children who hold only Japanese citizenship but who don't look very Japanese are classified as belonging to another culture or country. Some refer to these children in the aggregate as "marginal man." To avoid teasing — which is as much of a problem here in Okinawa as it is on mainland Japan — many parents of biracial children send them to the Christian schools, the private ones where there are other students like them, allowing the kids to feel some sense of belonging.

Another problem concerns language. Should these children speak English, Japanese, or both? Back in the early postwar period when Okinawa was desperately poor, a lot of mothers with biracial children wanted their kids to speak only English. See, at that time the Okinawans felt like backward and unsophisticated people compared with the Americans. In their minds, America was a superior place, a country with better and richer people. So naturally they wanted their children to learn English. Even though the mothers could hardly speak English themselves, they tried to use it exclusively around their children. A lot of women still think that way these days, but others insist the reason they speak only one language with the child is because two languages would cause too much confusion. Since most of the military men here don't speak Japanese, the Okinawan women end up speaking English at home with their families.

It's funny how we refer to these children born of parents from two different cultures. Some people call them *kokusaiji* [international child], or *konketsuji* [child of mixed blood]. I don't think either one of these terms is appropriate. After all, in the case of the first word, it sounds too much like *kokusaijin* [international/cosmopolitan person]. Are we suggesting by the use of this word that the child will grow up to be a *kokusaijin?* Don't get me wrong, there's nothing bad about the word *kokusaijin,* but I don't think it should be used for children born of parents from two different cultures. It's not an accurate distinction.

You know, biracial children aren't the only ones who have troubles in Okinawan society. Their parents, too, have all sorts of problems to deal with. One thing I could never understand is where we got the term *kokusai kekkon* [international marriage] to refer to a union of people from two different cultures. Are we suggesting this kind of marriage is more like a partnership between countries than people? This makes me feel that if I married someone from a different country and we had marital problems, we needn't blame ourselves. Just let our two countries take responsibility. After all, it *is* an international marriage! I think we should refer to marriages as marriages. That's natural, isn't it? Why the distinction?

In the States a marriage between people from two different countries is referred to as a cross-cultural marriage or a transcultural marriage. I think those are more accurate terms than the ones we use here in Okinawa and on mainland Japan. Americans tend to look at the culture of a person as opposed to that person's nationality or race. I wish we'd start doing that in Okinawa.

Cross-cultural marriages aren't easy. Whenever I'm involved in premarital counseling sessions, I talk with the Okinawan women about divorce. What a strange thing to talk about to women who are excited to get married, right? Well, sometimes they don't think about the tremendous cultural differences that exist, and are just carried away with the thought of getting married. I'm there to let them know what sorts of problems they may encounter and to challenge them to consider whether or not they can handle those issues. I let them know that Americans see things differently from Japanese, and that this may cause conflict in the marriage. The women need to understand right from the start that things might not be perfect.

Over the years I've counseled a lot of couples here. And I've heard many of the same complaints. In most cases the man is stationed here with the military and starts dating a local girl. Often the girl becomes pregnant, and the couple marries only to discover that they're incompatible. Some divorce, but others come here seeking counseling. Often the counseling sessions turn into a "He said, she said," situation with each person blaming the other. We act as interpreters, not only linguistic interpreters, but also culture and value interpreters. We tell the woman that if a man does or says such-and-such, it doesn't necessarily mean something bad; in America that's just the way things are. And we tell the man that certain things his wife may say aren't necessarily negative, but rather a reflection of the society in which she was raised.

Most of the problems between these couples center around money. A case I remember clearly involved a fight over baby pictures. See, in Okinawa, when a baby turns one hundred days old, the parents take the child to a photographer to get formal pictures taken. It's a tradition here on the island to get these portraits done. Well, a couple came to the office one day asking for our help because the American husband refused to pay for those pictures. He kept telling his wife, "I'll just borrow a camera from a friend and take the pictures myself. Then my buddy can develop them. Why should we spend three hundred dollars for formal shots?" Well, the wife got upset because she wanted the photos done professionally. The couple couldn't resolve the problem by themselves, so they came here to the office. We talked with the American man for a long time and tried to explain just how precious those baby pictures are to Okinawan mothers. After a while he softened up. "Well, I don't like it," he insisted, "but if that's the way things are here, then I guess I have to go along with it." Everything worked out in the end for that couple.

Sometimes things aren't so easily resolved, though. Lots of American men who come here for counseling with their wives think we're siding with the women and aren't trying to see the male interpretation of the situation. And if the wives go to counseling services on the bases, they complain that the counselors there side with the men. So we came to the conclusion that the ideal situation was one in which all four people — the couple, a Japanese social worker, and an American social worker — sat down together in the same room and attempted to resolve the problem. Many people didn't like this arrangement in the end, though. They thought it wasn't necessary to have so many people involved. *She sighed.*

This may sound stereotypical, but a lot of these men who marry Okinawan women are the type of guys who haven't had much luck with females back in the States. They come over here to Asia with the military and never want to leave. They're suddenly filled with confidence and approach girls more easily than they did back home. In many cases they marry a local girl and then think she's going to be quiet and subservient and docile. I think they expect a geisha or something. *She forced a smile.* One of the reasons many American men believe this is because when we Okinawans first start dating someone, we're shy and reserved. I was that way with my husband, too. It's just our nature to be like that. But as we get to know someone, we change. I think that's when the man becomes disillusioned and feels threatened by the woman when at one time he felt like he was her hero or protector.

I think some of the most complicated cases I've had to deal with here over the years involve women who get pregnant by men they barely know and then come to the center hoping we can make contact with the guys. Naturally they want the men to take responsibility as fathers. Well, often when we ask these women for information about the men such as a name, birthday, or social security number, they tell us things like, "His name's Sam Houston, and he's from Texas," or "I think he lives somewhere near the entrance to Gate Three of such-and-such base." Well, how are we supposed to locate men that way? And so the women end up having the babies and receiving some assistance from the Japanese government, but none from the fathers of the children.

Before reversion in 1972 a lot of women in this situation gave their babies up for adoption because they couldn't afford to take care of them. That was back when Okinawa was under U.S. occupation (1945 to 1972), and we weren't able to get the same governmental medical assistance and benefits that the mainland Japanese could. After all, we weren't considered part of Japan at that time. Plus, there wasn't a lot of aid for single-parent households in those days. So, naturally things here were hard economically speaking. People don't realize that a lot of children were given up for adoption at that time for financial reasons, not necessarily racial ones.

There haven't been many cases of adoption at the center recently. About one or two a year. People are better off economically now than they were thirty years ago. Plus they have medical insurance and can take care of their children. But some women here still try to get financial assistance from the fathers of their babies, especially if they were once married to the men. The women who face problems are the ones who had babies out of wedlock. See, in the States you have the Privacy Act, which prevents people from acquiring certain information about an individual. If an Okinawan woman had been married to an American man, that's different; we have the right to certain information about him in those cases. But for those women who were never married to the men, things are harder. There's less we can do for them in terms of making contact with the guy.

Another problem arises if a married couple divorces, and the court determines that the man has to provide child support to the woman. Often the American man thinks it doesn't cost anything to raise a child. After all, in the States it's cheap. Compulsory education is free, and clothes and food are inexpensive. In Okinawa, though, things are pricey. It's one thing if the man is Michael Jackson or someone who can pay for these things, but most of these guys aren't rich; they're in the military. So the women and children suffer.

You know, though, Okinawan women have survived pretty well over the years. They're really strong. In fact, I think we're stronger and more independent than the women on the mainland. A lot more Okinawan women work, for example. I guess that's because so many of our men were killed during the war that the women had to take jobs to feed their families. So, during the postwar years, people like me grew up seeing women in positions of responsibility, holding serious jobs. Also, it's more convenient for women to work here in Okinawa than on the mainland because they don't have to travel very far, and they can entrust their children to their parents or sisters to watch. On the mainland, though, everyone has to travel so far on the train to get to work. And husbands work so late that women need to be at home to take care of the kids and keep the household in order. Plus, daycare on the mainland is so expensive.

Another difference between Okinawan women and women from mainland Japan concerns the way we view marriage. On the mainland women can call counseling centers if they're having marital problems and need some advice. The counselors usually tell the women to stay with their men for financial reasons or to stick it out for the sake of the kids. That kind of talk makes us laugh here in Okinawa. Our counselors tell you to divorce. Why put up with a bad marital situation? Maybe that's why the divorce rate in Okinawa is so high.[5] It's the highest in Japan. Women in Okinawa feel they can make it on their own because they have a lot of support here. Families are generally large and *yuruyaka* [lenient and easygoing]; people help one another out. Plus, it's easy for women to work here since Okinawa is a service-centered economy. Women can always find some sort of office work or part-time job. And, unlike the mainland, the culture in Okinawa is less of a shame culture. Here we aren't so embarrassed by the fact that we may have a child and not be married.

Unfortunately most people, including mainlanders, don't know much about the Okinawans and our lifestyle and customs. That's not unusual I guess. I mean, there's geographical distance as well as psychological distance from the mainland. Think about the States. Do the people in New York know much about the social conditions of people in New Mexico?

In the future I'd like to write a book about my life experiences as an Okinawan. In fact, a group of female friends and I have been thinking about doing this for a long time now, compiling our life stories into a book. We're all about the same age and have the same sense of values, but our lives are so different. Some of us married foreigners, and others Japanese. Some women worked throughout their lifetimes, while others were housewives. It's interesting how individuals' lives turn out, don't you think? That's why we're anxious to put something together, a women's history of sorts, to let people know what life was like for us here during the past half century.

I'll have some time to work on this project when my job here at the center finishes up in March. I can't believe I've been here for thirty years. Time flies. Looking back on things, I feel a great sense of satisfaction with my professional life. After all, I had the opportunity to use the skills I learned in school in my professional career. For example, I studied English at Waseda, and social work in the States. My job here at the welfare center allowed me to combine these skills to help other people. I feel good because of that.

I guess I've thought about going far away from the island on occasion. You know, taking the time after I retire to travel to foreign countries. I've always wanted to go to Africa or to Europe. Before I do any of that, though, I'd like to take a sentimental journey, a trip to Tokyo to visit my old haunts: Waseda University, the places where I protested during the 60s, and the areas of the city where I hung out as a college student. Of course, part of this sentimental journey will involve going to the States as well. Back to Buffalo where I studied as a graduate student. It'll be interesting to look at those places thirty years later and see how much my impressions have changed, if at all. Will things look the same to me? Will I remember those places with nostalgia? I guess I won't know until I get there, right? That's when I'll realize how much things change, and how much they remain the same.

6 : NOBUKO KARIMATA

The city bus deposited me at the corner of Kokusai Dōri *(International Street) near the Prefectural Government Office* (kenchō). *I waited as the long blue-and-white steel bus with the jumbo rubber tires coughed away from the curb and wheezed through the intersection before crossing the busy street and heading west. I walked in search of the Okinawa Women's Comprehensive Center, the venue for my interview with Nobuko Karimata, the director.*

The Center is located at the far end of Naminoue, the famed red-light district of the Occupation era. The section had a suburban feel to it, the tree-lined streets perhaps responsible for the residential flavor. As I traveled deeper into the heart of the area, the atmosphere changed; architectural residue from the 1950s hinted at the area's licentious heritage. Walking along, stretching my neck around animatedly, I tried to absorb all of the sights in the area: the faded bar signs, the defunct corner diner with the red vinyl stools, and the dismal dazzle of the bulbous white lights adorning the entrance of a 1950s-style cabaret. The only sign of life in the area that afternoon was a middle-aged woman with cherry-red lips who appeared from nowhere and stared at me as I sauntered down the middle of the street. When I looked over my shoulder to catch another glimpse of her, she scowled. Then she darted into a doorway and vanished inside.

As quickly as I happened upon Naminoue, I escaped from it. Suddenly I was on the outskirts of the district and, once again, a part of the 1990s. I found the Comprehensive Center with few problems and waited patiently at the front desk to speak with Karimata-san. The reception-

ist led me into a spacious room with slate-gray leather sofas and toast-colored carpet. The place looked new, untouched. I learned later that the facility was just two years old.

Karimata-san breezed into the conference room within minutes of my arrival, her meishi *(business card) held between the fingertips of her right hand. She wore a black-and-white hound's-tooth checkered blazer, black slacks, and a fuchsia silk scarf around her neck. Her lipstick matched the hue of her scarf. Her jet-black hair was styled in a pageboy coiffure, with short bangs and iron-straight sides.*

During our talks, Karimata-san, the 57-year-old managing director of the Okinawa Women's Foundation and the director of the Okinawa Women's Comprehensive Center, shared with me her reasons for becoming such a vocal and enthusiastic proponent of women's rights and equality between the sexes. Devotion to these issues, she insists, stems from childhood and her recollections of constant disparity between the sexes on an island heavily influenced by tradition and rooted in patriarchal devotion. Karimata-san did not limit our discussion to gender-related issues; she also talked about her involvement in the island's powerful Teachers Association[1] (Kyōshokuiinkai) *and the issues the Association faced throughout the postwar period, especially during the pre-reversion years, as Okinawans strived to achieve equality with the mainland Japanese.*

"The Americans are coming! The Americans are coming! Hide!" That's what we used to scream when we heard the clang of the village bell. Gan-gan-gan-gan, *Karimata-san mimicked the sound.* I can still hear the shrill sound of that bell to this day.

In the immediate postwar years, there was a huge bell in each village. If it rang once, that meant there was a meeting in town. If it rang continuously, that signaled a problem, namely that an American soldier was in the neighborhood. Sometimes the soldiers entered residential areas to rape women. In fact, there were so many cases of rape in those early postwar years that whenever we spotted an American on our streets, we thought for sure he was a rapist. The GIs usually ran away when they heard the sound of the bell, but sometimes they just hid in the village until things calmed down. This went on from the end of the war in 1945 until around 1950 or so. After that, things started to settle down.

The first time I ever saw an American was when I returned to Okinawa from Gifu Prefecture[2] on the mainland. My mother and sisters and I were evacuated there during the war. My father didn't go with us since he had to stay behind in Okinawa to work in the Home Guard. He didn't want to stay here on the island, but he was forced to. Fortunately he survived the war unharmed.

When we docked in Naha, I found myself face to face with a black American GI. What a shock! I had no idea people could have skin that color. After all, I was just a 5-year-old girl. What did I know? I remember staring at that soldier as I stepped off the boat. Didn't say a word. He took my mother, my sisters, and me aside and sprayed us with DDT from head to toe. Everyone on the boat was sprayed since so many of us Okinawans had lice during wartime. After that we were permitted to leave, so we headed off to find my father. We heard he was living in a place called Yorimia in Naha. He knew we were on our way home to Okinawa because he saw our names on a list of people scheduled to be repatriated from the mainland.

I didn't have much contact with Americans after that even though the island was under American occupation from the time I was 5 years old until I reached 31. But I remember being afraid of the military guys. I used to see them walking down *Kokusai Dōri* [International Street] covered in tattoos, or hanging out on the streets of Koza [Okinawa City] in those gaudy jackets with designs of tigers or snakes on the back. That was during the 1960s. All of the GIs were so wild at that time, so full of nervous energy. Lots of them were here for R&R [rest and relaxation] from Vietnam. That's when the crime rate skyrocketed on the island. Most of the trouble occurred in Koza. The streets up there were segregated: one area for whites, and another for blacks. If a white guy went over to the black area, he was beaten up. And, likewise, if a black guy entered white territory, he was beaten up. Seemed like we were always hearing about bar fights and robberies, rapes and traffic violations in that area.

I guess what angered us Okinawans the most was that the GIs used to get away with a lot of the crimes they committed against the local citizenry. All they had to do was run inside the confines of the military bases where we couldn't arrest them. Kind of like running away at the sound of the village bell, huh? If they managed to get caught and put on trial in a military court, they were almost always acquitted. *She sighed as she shook her head back and forth.* Everything from a traffic violation to a rape resulted in the same verdict: innocent. Incidents like these were what encouraged us to campaign so vehemently for reversion to Japan. Can you blame us?

One of the groups on the island that was really active in campaigning for reversion was the Okinawa Teachers Association. In the immediate postwar years the Association's main goal was to resurrect the educational system in Okinawa because it'd been completely destroyed during the war. The members of the Association wanted to give the students in Okinawa the same educational opportunities the children on the mainland had. They used to petition the mainlanders for teaching materials and supplies to use in the classrooms here. We didn't have anything in Okinawa, not even the resources to print our own textbooks. So we had to ask the mainland Japanese to send those as well.

The first shipment of books from the mainland were ones used in the prewar period, so they were filled with anti-democratic and militaristic propaganda. The teachers here had to take ink and cover over those parts of the books before letting the students use them! See, the American Occupation government was trying to promote democracy in Okinawa, so they carefully censored everything we were reading at the time to make sure it was appropriate. Obviously those prewar textbooks weren't. Eventually new textbooks were printed, and we got a shipment of them here on the island. They're the ones I remember using as a kid.

By the time I became involved in the Teachers Association in the late 1960s, the educational system here on Okinawa still lagged behind the one on the mainland. We didn't have the same facilities the schools up there did, such as pools, gyms, and scientific equipment for experiments. So we continued to campaign for access to things the mainland children had and the Okinawan kids didn't. Even today Okinawa isn't on par with the mainland. But we're catching up.

I guess the most important issue for the Association during the 1960s, though, was *fukki undō* [campaigns for reversion]. The Association wasn't the only group on the island that devoted its energy to this cause; almost all organized groups here, including university student groups, made reversion one of the main issues on their agendas. We were sick of the American Occupation on the island, and tired of lagging behind mainland Japan both educationally and economically. After all, we're Japanese, so it was only natural we'd want to be reunited with the motherland, not to mention legally protected by the Japanese Constitution. Instead, we were living on an island occupied by an American military government and overrun with U.S. bases. It was terrible. You know, young people today can't understand the frustration we felt at the time since they didn't experience life here during those twenty-seven years of occupation. But for the people who lived through those years, life was unbearable. The Americans took over our land, denied us our rights, and got away with all sorts of crimes. It was only natural that we campaigned for reversion to Japan. Some islanders even suggested Okinawa would be better off if it were independent. They didn't think Okinawa needed the Americans *or* the Japanese in order to survive.

Well, on May 15, 1972, we Okinawans got what we wished for: Okinawa reverted to Japanese rule. Unfortunately it wasn't the reversion we had hoped for. We thought once the Occupation ended, the U.S. bases would disappear from the island. That was wishful thinking. The bases remained, and discrimination against the Okinawans continued. The only thing that changed after reversion was that we were suddenly included under the Japanese Constitution and could enjoy the same rights as people on the mainland. Other than that, though, things stayed the same on Okinawa. Needless to say, we were disappointed. We felt like we'd been betrayed again by the mainland Japanese.

After reversion, the Association didn't stop struggling for change. One of the issues that got our attention in the 1980s concerned textbooks issued by *Monbushō* [Japanese Ministry of Education]. Previously, facts about World War II weren't reported accurately or honestly in our textbooks. Japan's militarism was glossed over, and the horrible acts of aggression the Japanese soldiers committed throughout Asia were ignored or misrepresented. That's when we started petitioning *Monbushō* to write about the war objectively. I mean, people should know about the sort of things Japan did during the war, right? Most Asians agreed with us Okinawans. People from Korea, especially, appealed to the Japanese government to report the war fairly and honestly. Little by little, the Japanese government started doing that. One person who was instrumental in getting these changes passed was a Japanese man named Saburo Ienaga. In the 1960s when he was a university president, he was active in compelling the government to record facts about the war. His struggle lasted thirty years. Now textbooks tell us the truth about the war. We'd like even more to be written, but, compared to before, it's a great improvement. In high school textbooks today, even information about the mass suicides that took place here, as well as the slaughter of innocent Okinawan citizens by Japanese soldiers, is reported.

Back in the days when I was a student, I didn't learn there were comfort women [women forced into prostitution] here in Okinawa or that some Japanese soldiers killed their own countrymen, the Okinawans, during battle. It was only after I became a teacher that I learned about these things. And, as a high school social studies instructor, I taught these facts to my students. Of course, *Monbushō* at the time didn't want me teaching such things, but I did anyhow. It's only right to teach the truth about history, isn't it?

Today we're still learning things about the war. In fact, ten years ago a group of women researchers did an investigation on the island and discovered that during the war there were 130 brothels here used by the Japanese military. Both Korean and Okinawan women were forced into prostitution for these men. Sometimes the Japanese soldiers even used private homes as brothels. Just came in and overtook the places. They had a lot of power at that time, the Japanese military. Of course during the Occupation period, the Americans, too, had their own brothels in Okinawa.[3]

Another big issue the Teachers Association concerned itself with in the 1980s was allegiance to the *Hinomaru* [Japanese flag] and the *Kimigayo* [Japanese anthem].[4] Personally, I've always believed that people should be free to decide for themselves whether or not to pay homage to the Japanese flag or to sing the *Kimigayo*. But *Monbushō* felt differently. They tried to force us teachers in Okinawa to play tapes of the *Kimigayo* at school in an effort to teach students the words to that song. In fact, they kept sending us tapes in the mail and telling us to play them at formal school ceremonies so that the students could get used to the words. That was around 1986, one year before the National Athletic Meet was scheduled to be held in Okinawa. Prior to 1986, they didn't pay too much attention to what we were doing down here.

The reason why the Japanese government, especially *Monbushō*, was worried about whether we Okinawans knew the words to the *Kimigayo* is simple. Each year a National Athletic Meet takes place in Japan, and in 1987 Okinawa was the venue. Well, *Monbushō* was anxious because they knew about the islanders' strong feelings of resistance to both the flag and the song. To Okinawans, the *Hinomaru* symbolizes Japan's martial past, a past in which Okinawa was sacrificed to protect the mainland. *Monbushō* officials didn't care about this, though; they wanted to see teachers here on the island promoting allegiance to both the flag and the song. I guess they were worried about being embarrassed at the Athletic Meet if the Okinawans refused to do these things. But many teachers here, including me, weren't willing to go along with this. I can't quietly agree with something if I feel deep down it isn't right.

On the day of the Athletic Meet, the *Hinomaru* was flown, and the *Kimigayo* was sung.[5] But not many Okinawans stood when the flag was being raised. Most of the people standing were mainland Japanese who'd come here to the island for the Athletic Meet.

I can't remember ever raising the flag back when I was a student. Come to think of it, I don't recall singing the *Kimigayo*, either. I knew the words to that song, though, because my mother used to sing it at the house. She grew up in the prewar era when they sang the *Kimigayo* at school, so of course she still remembered the lyrics. The words to that song are words of reverence to the Emperor. That's why we Okinawans today are against it. That's only natural, isn't it, considering our history?

After serving as President of the island's High School Teachers Labor Union[6] *from 1994 to 1996, Karimata-san was invited by the Okinawan Prefectural Government to head the newly built Women's Comprehensive Center. For the past two years, Karimata-san has worked as director of this center, struggling to remedy gender-based inequities in Okinawan society. She talks about how she became interested in women's issues, and why she has chosen to devote so much time and effort to the fight for sexual equality on the island.*

When I was growing up, I always felt like men were treated specially in this society. For example, when my mother was pregnant with one of my sisters, the women in the neighborhood kept telling her, "Have a boy! Have a boy!" As if she could control what sex the child was! At that time I couldn't understand why everyone was so eager for her to have a baby boy. I realize now they were worried that my parents weren't going to have an heir, someone to take care of the *ihai* [ancestral tablets] after my mother and father passed away. This responsibility generally goes to a son. Well, my mother disappointed the neighborhood women by giving birth to another girl. She had eight children in total. All girls. She kept having baby after baby, waiting for a boy.

I never understood why the *ihai* had to pass to a male child. What's wrong with girls? Why can't they inherit their parents' property and the *ihai* just like boys? I guess those sorts of questions influenced me to study more about gender-related issues in this society. In fact, I entered Ryukyu University in 1963 to study law. I wanted to use what I learned in school to change society, to make conditions more equal for men and women. At that time, law was a man's world. Women were expected to study things like Japanese literature, music, and home economics. My mother and father didn't tell me I should study one of those subjects, though. They encouraged my sisters and me to do whatever we wanted to do. In fact, my parents thought I'd make a good lawyer since I was such a talker. *She laughed.* I ended up becoming a teacher, though, not a lawyer. I don't think I consciously intended to do that. I just happened to take the prefectural teachers' exam during my senior year, and when I heard I'd passed, I decided to go into teaching. But that doesn't mean I gave up on my former dream of improving gender relations in this society. In fact, that's exactly what I'm hoping to do right now at this center.

The Women's Comprehensive Center was created in 1996. Leaders of women's organizations throughout the island had been discussing the need for a center like this one for quite a few years. Then, when Masahide Ota was elected governor in 1990, the plan to build the Women's Comprehensive Center became a reality.

The main aim of the Center is to change traditional ideas about the roles men and women are expected to play in society. For years women in Okinawa have been oppressed. It's about time they're seen as men's equals. Women play a beneficial role in many professional fields, just like men do. But most of the time they aren't recognized for it. That's why we try to increase people's awareness of the ways in which women are discriminated against both personally and professionally in Okinawa.

We begin by discussing inequality within the household. For instance, why don't more couples share domestic responsibilities? Why is it that women have to cook and clean and do laundry even when they're tired from working all day? Can't the guys help out? Actually, young Okinawan men are probably a little better than the older generation of men on this island. Would you believe there are some old men in this society who can't even make rice? They just wait around for their wives or daughters to do it. That's not right. Here at the Center, we started holding cooking classes for men. They've been a real hit, right from the start. Most of the men who come to the classes are young guys; some married, some single. It's a good trend, in my opinion, to see the young generation of males making an effort to take responsibility at home.

Outside the home, too, there's still a lot of discrimination against females. Take the field of politics for instance. Why aren't there more women in positions of power in the government, or on local councils? It shouldn't have to be so difficult for women in Okinawa to break through the male barrier and gain positions in politics. The first time a female attained a high office here was in 1991 when Hiroko Sho became the vice-governor. She was the first female vice-governor on the island. I think it'll be a long time before we see a female governor, though. Women will probably have to be a part of the Diet [Japanese Parliament] before they can run for the position of governor here.

Even though this Center is young, I think we've been successful in getting things accomplished so far. We've had hundreds of seminars and workshops for individuals and groups, and we've counseled lots of Okinawan couples who've come here for assistance. Most of the problems they're dealing with are the same sorts of problems couples in other countries have — things like incompatibility, financial difficulties, and communication problems with their children. We've even handled cases of sexual harassment and rape. We have a lawyer, a doctor, and a psychologist on staff here, as well as four professionally trained counselors, to help us solve these problems. Many of the problems are the result of tradition; men think things should be a certain way and refuse to change. Because of this, women suffer.

Gender-related problems in this country aren't limited to Okinawa. In fact, there are probably more problems between the sexes on mainland Japan since it's a *tate shakai* [vertical society] up there, one in which people are concerned about rank and position. And usually men are at the top of those rankings. For example, when I went to a conference on the mainland once, I asked a few women, "Who gets in the bath first at your house, the men or the women?" As you know, we all use the same bath water in the home.[7] All of the mainland women said the bath order began with the oldest man, such as the grandfather, followed by the father and then the sons. When they finished, the women got in the tub. In my home, the person who wants to get in the bath first can get in first; there's no special order. That's only normal I think. Why should everyone sit around waiting to get in the bath if, for example, the father of the house is working late? If my husband had had a rule like this at our house, I would've taken off a long time ago. "Sayonara!" I'd shout as I walked out the door. *She laughed.*

And in certain rural areas of the mainland, some women still don't sit with their families at the dinner table; they kneel in the corner and wait on their husband and children hand and foot. We'd never think of doing that in Okinawa! At least not in the postwar period. In the prewar years, though, there were similar discriminatory customs here, all of which were introduced from the mainland a couple hundred years ago. For example, men always got to sit at the best spot around the kitchen table, and they were served their meal before everyone else. But after the war, lots of dramatic changes took place on the island. See, everything here was destroyed during wartime, so men and women had to work side by side to rebuild the country after 1945. That's when men recognized that women could do the same things they could do. Many of them stopped thinking they were better than women and started to see both sexes as equal.

Not everyone's way of thinking changed, though. If it had, there wouldn't be a need for a center like this one, right? For good or for bad, traditions on the island are strong, deeply ingrained in people's minds and hearts. That's why some men here have such a hard time doing things they think are traditionally female tasks. They're stubborn. Thankfully my husband doesn't have a problem with helping me out around the house. We were both looking for an equal partnership when we married, which is why we haven't had any marital problems. He's terrific about cooking and even doing his own laundry. If he didn't, it'd just stay dirty for days because often I don't have the time to do it!

My husband and I got married in 1970. We met back in high school and dated for eleven years before we tied the knot. I can't count how many times he proposed to me before I finally accepted. I guess I was worried about losing my independence after marriage, afraid of being confined to the house if I had children. Well, he waited for me. As I approached 30 years old, I had to start thinking seriously about having kids because my biological clock was ticking. So, at 29 I got married, and I had my first child at 30.

My marriage is nothing like that of my parents. I grew up watching my mother listen to whatever my father said. That turned me off. But, I guess I couldn't blame her; she was raised during the Meiji era when women were supposed to be subservient to their husbands. I knew I didn't want to be that way with my husband. And I'm not.

Some men on the island have a problem with females like me who challenge tradition. "Women like you are tough to deal with," they tease. Not really. What's wrong with wanting to see things change here? What's wrong with trying to achieve improvement in the status of women? Of course I'm interested in seeing progress in relations between men and women on Okinawa, but I'm also interested in seeing advancement in the position of women around the world. So many women still live in poverty and have no rights. That's not fair. As a woman and as a human being I can't feel emancipated knowing that other females around the world don't enjoy the basic rights men enjoy. I guess that's why I try so hard to alter people's ways of thinking and to break down traditions that hurt, not help, women in society.

One of the reasons I'm so passionate in trying to get things changed is because I'm a product of the 1960s, a generation when we young adults on the island were constantly demonstrating, if not against the U.S. military bases, then for the island's return to Japan. Things weren't stable at that time; there was always some sort of struggle going on. A lot of today's young people don't understand the struggles of the past. They grew up in a relatively stable society, far removed from the problems that people of my generation had to deal with. There are some young people on the island, though, who are socially conscious. They're the ones who've been influenced by their families, their jobs, or their education to work for change in this society. But, unfortunately, the majority of young people here don't appear too interested in the problems facing women in Okinawa. Maybe as they grow older they'll change? I don't know. I'd like to see them continue the struggle that women of my generation got involved in. After all, if they don't take up the challenge, who will?

CONTEMPORARY OKINAWAN WOMEN

Route 58 in downtown Naha City, the island's capital.
The highway was built by U.S. troops during the early years of the
American Occupation.

Sign at an American army base in Yomitan-son, Okinawa-ken. Civilians are not permitted inside the gates of a military facility without permission and an escort.

Gate Two Street, outside Kadena Air Base in north-central Okinawa. On the left, taxi drivers wait for a fare. An elderly woman strolls along the street, and two American GIs in civilian clothing head east toward the main highway.

Kin Village, near Hansen Marine Base in northern Okinawa.
Okinawan mothers and their children pass an Occupation-era tailor's shop.

Maiko Sunabe and her grandmother prepare traditional foods in front of the family
tomb in Yomitan-son, Okinawa-ken. At seimei, *in late April and early May, family*
members gather at the ancestral grave site to pay homage to deceased relatives.

An American GI shops for jewelry with his companion on Park Avenue (formerly BC Street) near Kadena Air Station. The sign in the foreground advertises "Diamonds."

Elderly Okinawan fisherman preparing his nets near Ikei-jima, Okinawa-ken.

Kokusai Dōri (International Street), in Naha City.
A storefront advertises dog tags and other military surplus goods.

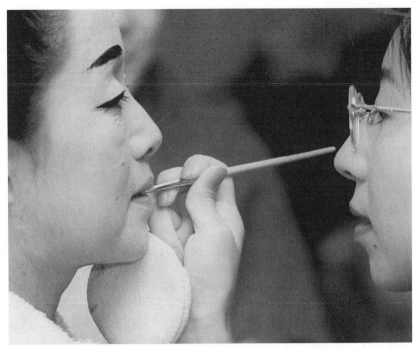

A makeup artist applies cherry-red lip coloring to a classical Ryukyuan dancer before a performance.

Ikei-jima, Okinawa-ken.
A girl wearing plastic slippers runs through the streets
on a hot summer morning.

Hamahigajima, Okinawa-ken.
An elderly islander in a straw hat walks home after
purchasing goods at a local store.

Tokashikijima, Okinawa-ken. Four elderly islanders stave off the humid summer weather. The character on the fan reads matsuri, *"festival."*

Futenma Marine Air Station in central Okinawa.
An elderly Okinawan woman wearing protective headgear cuts the lawn.
Barbed-wire fencing separates the American military
from the Okinawan populace.

7 : MARIKO HIGA

I met Mariko Higa[1] for the first time at her apartment in Urasoe City, located several miles from the capital, Naha, in the southern part of the island. Mariko-san's American husband, Ken, had invited me to dine with him, his wife, and his stepson, Shuichi, Mariko-san's 10-year-old son from a previous marriage.

"I'd like you to meet my wife," Ken had suggested weeks earlier when I met with him on the U.S. military base where he works. "She's Okinawan and might be willing to share with you her thoughts about growing up in this society."

So, one Sunday evening in November I joined them at their home for dinner. Their apartment is grand, with big, spacious rooms and a wide balcony that commands a beautiful view of the capital. Ken was standing in the kitchen when I arrived, busily chopping green peppers and dicing onions for the spaghetti sauce.

"Take a seat," he offered, pointing his free hand toward one of the heavy wooden chairs positioned around the kitchen table. "Mariko'll be home soon. She just went to pick up our son."

I sat down and glanced around the apartment, admiring the hardwood floors and the overstuffed American-style couches and chunky wooden end tables. Ken and I chatted for awhile until his wife arrived.

The hinge on the screen door squeaked as she pulled it open.

"Hi!" Mariko-san grinned as she held her hand behind her to keep the thin metal door from slamming shut. "I'm Mariko, and this is my son, Shuichi." She approached the kitchen table where I was seated and shook my hand. Shuichi greeted me with a nod of the head and

"konnichiwa" *(hello) before dragging his suitcases and duffel bags from the living room into his bedroom to unpack. Shuichi divides his time equally between his father and mother's homes, rotating back and forth every other month. He was planning to spend the next month with Mariko-san and Ken.*

Mariko-san disappeared into the bedroom to change her clothes, returning in minutes clad in a pair of gray sweat pants and a white T-shirt. Plopping down on one of the kitchen chairs, she pulled her knees up against her chest, then reached back to tie her inky black hair in a ponytail. She lit a cigarette from the white pack in front of her, exhaled slowly, and asked her husband what was for dinner.

He recited the menu, and she smiled.

"He's great," she said. "He always cooks."

Mariko Higa is a beautiful, 35-year-old Okinawan woman with large brown almond-shaped eyes, a round face, and a beamish smile. She is employed at one of the U.S. military installations on the island as a secretary. She has been working in base-related jobs for four years. Through our numerous conversations during my year on Okinawa, she shared her impressions of life as a woman on the island during the past thirty years, including her memories of friendships with American soldiers, her reflections on marriage and motherhood, and her feelings about working on a U.S. military base. She also talked about the elements of Okinawan society she would like to see changed, from discrimination within the workplace to people's attitudes toward the American military presence on the island. Before beginning our discussion Mariko-san reminded me she is not a typical Okinawan. "I don't necessarily think like the rest of the people on the island," she confessed the evening we first met. Then she inquired playfully, "Are you still interested in hearing my life story?"

We began our conversation around the kitchen table that evening after dinner. She prepared two large mugs of coffee, placing one in front of me as she took her seat. As she stirred sugar and powdered creamer into her coffee, she looked toward me and asked,

Have you ever worked for a Japanese company? For a woman, it's a terrible experience. I worked at a major Japanese radio station in Okinawa as a disc jockey from 1982 to 1985. All I did was prepare coffee and tea and listen to the men harass me. "Why don't you wear shorter skirts?" they'd ask. Or, "Why are you covering up your breasts? Wear something tighter so we can see them." I used to hate that, but it's normal behavior in this society. Some women played cutesy and acted like they were angry when the men grabbed their breasts, but they really weren't. So the men just continued doing it. It was like a big game. And the worst part is that the men didn't think of it as sexual harassment.

At this company, we women had to arrive thirty minutes ahead of schedule in the morning to wash the tea and *sake* cups. Every time they took a drink, the men used a fresh cup. That's because they didn't have to do the washing. The women always used the same cup throughout the day and rinsed it out before leaving. But the guys drank tea and *sake* all day long, then left a sink full of dirty dishes for us to clean up. I used to get angry about this, especially when I was busy with other work. "Why can't the men help out?" I wanted to scream. But I never said anything. I don't know what good it would've done. *She shrugged.* I stayed at that job for three years. I never got to say much on the air since I was only an assistant disc jockey. I just threw out things like "Oh, really?" and "Isn't that interesting?" when the main male announcer did his show on the air.

Before accepting a job offer at a Japanese company, we women aren't told we have to do things like make tea, wash dishes, and arrange flowers around the office. But once we start working, we notice other women are doing those sorts of things and are being praised. The men say things like, "Oh, she's a good girl, isn't she?" or, "Oh she's really feminine!" So lots of women continue to perform these tasks without complaint. That's just part of our culture here, I guess.

Fortunately I haven't felt any discrimination working on the American military bases. People there are so serious. I mean, they do their jobs without bothering anyone else. I like that. And the men there have good manners. For example, they open doors for women and carry heavy things for them if they see the women struggling. Japanese men would never think of doing that. They just let women fend for themselves. Plus, on base I don't have to make coffee and tea for the men I work with; everybody prepares their own. And the men even wash out their own cups before they leave for the day.

Another thing I like about working on base is the atmosphere. It's more relaxed than at a Japanese company. For example, the Americans aren't so concerned about throwing *enkai* [banquets, parties] that everyone has to attend. When the Americans have work-related parties, people come and go freely from them; they're meant to be fun. But *enkai* at Japanese companies have a pattern to them: the women spend half the night rushing around filling up men's glasses with beer or *sake,* and then everyone's forced to sing karaoke. Really, some people don't like karaoke, but they're pressured to sing anyhow. I can't stand that. And if someone tries to sneak out of the party early, everyone starts asking questions. "Where are you going?" "Why are you leaving so soon?" At an American party, though, it's no one's business where you're going; you're free to leave when you want. And Americans aren't so wrapped up in role playing and watching one another to see how to do something. They're independent. I respect that. Maybe that's why I feel a lot more comfortable around Americans than I do around Okinawans.

Most of us on base like the Americans we work with. But, of course, there are some Okinawans who complain about the Americans all the time. They say they're noisy and cheap. See, if there's a job to be done on base and the Americans decide to contract out, they always sign a contract with the company that has the most reasonable rates. Personally I think that's just one of the laws of business, but lots of Okinawans I work with think it's because the Americans are tightfisted. And, on top of that, when the contractors arrive at the office to do their job, the Okinawans complain that the Americans stand over them to make sure they're doing it properly.

Other Okinawans who work on base grumble about the space the bases take up, and how our island is overrun with military facilities. Then the next day they drive through the gates of the base, do their jobs alongside the Americans, use the golf and recreational facilities, and leave for the day — always at a reasonable hour. Honestly, it seems like some people in this society just can't think consistently. *She shook her head from side to side.*

I don't think I ever gave much thought to working on base. It just happened that way. A friend of mine saw a notice in the paper about a job opening in a communications-related position on one of the U.S. military bases. Since I'd been involved in similar work at the radio station, I thought I'd apply. There were two people hired for the job, and I was one of them.

When I took the job I was afraid I might feel some discrimination from other Okinawans for working on base. There are plenty of people here on the island who think it's wrong to work there. In fact, I have a friend who works on base, and one day she found a piece of paper taped to her car windshield that read, "*hikokumin*" [traitor]. Our cars are really visible because we have stickers on them identifying us as base workers. I couldn't believe when she told me about that incident. Nothing like that has ever happened to me. In fact, my family and friends were happy for me when I got a job on base. My mother was so proud. She kept bragging to everyone that her daughter spoke English well and had managed to secure a good job with the Americans.

My mother didn't work outside the home while I was growing up. She stayed at home and raised kids while my father worked. She never even finished high school. See, her family was really poor. Her mother — my grandmother — was a bar lady. She'd been sold by her parents to a family in Naha when she was in elementary school and spent her childhood years there working in the bar the family owned. I wish I could tell you exactly what she did at the bar, but we never talked about that at home. We think she worked as a geisha, you know, pouring drinks and playing the *sanshin* for male guests. My grandmother was a famous beauty when she was young, so it was normal in those days for girls like her to work in bars and restaurants that catered to men.

My grandmother never married, but she was a mistress to a certain man and had three children by him. My mother was one of those children. That man wanted to marry my grandmother, but his family had already arranged a marriage for him with a schoolteacher. They were of the same social standing, so it was logical that he married someone like her, not a bar lady like my grandmother. So Grandmom ended up raising the children alone. Things were tough for her. That's why my mother had to help out financially by quitting school in ninth grade and taking a job. She worked in a quilt shop. She stayed with that job until she married my father, who was one of her classmates at junior high school. I think she was surprised he liked her because she always thought a handsome, smart athlete like him was out of her reach!

I don't remember too much about my father since he died from a cerebral hemorrhage back when I was 13 years old. There are two things about him, though, I'll never forget. First, he used to tell my sisters and me never to marry an American or a mainland Japanese. Oh yeah, or a man from Miyako! [Miyako is one of the islands in the Okinawan archipelago.] He wanted to see us marry someone from right here on the main island of Okinawa. I guess you could say he was a bit of a racist. Second, my father always encouraged my two sisters and me to go to college. He didn't seem to care if my brothers went because he believed boys were able to take care of themselves in society. Girls, he claimed, would be buried in society without an education. So my sisters and I went to junior college. My two brothers never did end up going.

When I was in high school, I didn't think too much about going to college. There were other things on my mind at the time. *She smiled bashfully.* See, I had gotten involved with an American man. He was a 26-year-old black marine I met at a club one night in Naha when my girlfriend and I went out dancing. My friend was afraid of the Americans, but I wasn't scared of them. It wasn't like I'd had a lot of contact with foreigners or anything while I was growing up. I lived in the capital, Naha, and there weren't many military bases there in the city. In fact, the only time I ever saw the Americans was when my family took car trips up north. The roads were always clogged with cars full of GIs heading to the beaches. They used to shout out their windows to us. "Hi!" they'd scream, waving their hands in the air. We smiled back and waved at them. I remember thinking how different they were from the Japanese since most Japanese wouldn't just say hello like that, even if they sat down next to you.

Anyhow, I always thought the Americans were friendly people, so I wasn't nervous when that marine approached me at the club in Naha. I'll never forget how handsome he was; a truly beautiful person. While we were dancing our first slow dance together he kissed me. What a kiss! *She closed her eyes in remembrance.* I'd never been kissed like that before. It was moist and soft, different from the Japanese guys whose kisses are so dry. I think that's because his lips were so full. We Japanese don't have lips like that.

This guy gave me his phone number, and I got in touch with him. I was scared to have him call me at home, which is why I didn't give him my number. We ended up seeing each other for a year. It was wonderful! I was 17 years old and completely enamored with him. I didn't study at all. I didn't even worry about going to college. I thought maybe we'd get married eventually since we were together all the time.

Of course my mother had no idea I was seeing him. I don't think she would've approved, which is why I kept the relationship a secret from her. My sister knew about the marine, though, because she drove me to Camp Kinser[2] to meet him the first time we went out. When we drove up to the gate and she saw him standing there, she turned to me and asked, *"Honki?"* [Are you serious?]. I think she was surprised to see a big, black American waiting for me.

Well, one day when I was visiting him in the barracks, the female Okinawan maid on staff approached me and asked if I knew he was married. I couldn't believe it! I mean, we'd been dating for a year already. And he even told me he loved me. I questioned him about what the maid had said, and he denied it. Then when I asked him how long he planned on staying in Okinawa, he said he was leaving the next month. Why on earth had he waited this long to tell me? Even though I was hurt, I kept on seeing him, right up until the day he left. You should've seen how I cried at the airport. He cried, too. He told me he didn't know yet where he'd be staying in the States, so he didn't have an address to give me. I believed him and waited patiently for him to write.

I never heard from him again. Before he left the island he told me something about a system within the Marine Corps whereby he was expected to return to Okinawa in three months for more training. So I held out hope he'd come back to the island. Of course he never did. Once in a while, I ran into his friends in the disco or at a bar. When I asked them for his address, they gave me a phony one. Only I didn't know it was fake. So I wrote once or twice only to get the letters back marked, "Return to sender. Address unknown." Then I asked any serviceman I could find about whether there was a system in the military that required the men to return to Okinawa after three months. I remember one guy laughing as he told me, "I'll bet you one hundred dollars he doesn't come back!" And he didn't. At that point I figured he probably was married after all.

So there I was, a high school graduate with no job and no prospects for college since I'd devoted all of my time, effort, and energy to being with him. Actually I had sent in one application to a junior college on the island a few months earlier. I wrote that I wanted to major in English. I guess I wanted to study English formally because of my relationship with that marine. When he left me, though, I wanted to forget everything about English. I was so hurt, so upset over that breakup. I even gave my friends all of the music tapes he'd made for me. I wanted to erase him from my mind.

Eventually I decided to enroll in the junior college here on the island. In fact, *she hesitated*, I even ended up marrying one of my professors. It's funny how my relationship with that professor started. See, I was taking a class he offered at night. When it was over, I used to study in one of the empty rooms while I waited for him to finish teaching his other course. Then I offered to drive him home. I used to call out from my car, "*Sensei*, do you need a ride?" And he always let me drive him to his apartment. Sometimes he even took me out to dinner. I wasn't interested in him in a romantic way; I just enjoyed talking with him. He was so intelligent.

Well, one rainy night he confessed to me in the car that he liked me. I almost crashed when I heard that. See, I didn't feel the same way about him. It probably seems strange, then, that I decided to marry him. I guess the easiest way to explain why I did is that I needed some discipline in my life, and I thought he could offer me that. Maybe I just didn't have much confidence in myself at the time. I don't know.

I was 22 years old when I got married. My husband was 42. He was the first person to introduce me to feminism. For him, though, it was only a theory; it was never practiced in our household. I was a typical Japanese housewife. I know a lot of people say that and make it sound wonderful, but it wasn't. I was so dependent on my husband, especially financially. And when you're dependent on someone financially, you're dependent on him mentally. I always felt guilty if I bought something for myself using his money. Most of the time I stayed at home and read. He had thousands of books. And he could explain anything to me. Sometimes he'd laugh if I didn't know something. "You mean you've never heard of such-and-such?" he'd ask incredulously. Then he'd explain it to me. I learned so much from him. He was a brilliant man.

He was also a sickly one. Just six months after we got married, we discovered he had cancer. I remember going to a nearby hospital to have him checked. Well, in Japan, doctors generally don't tell a patient if he has cancer. It's a cultural thing. They prefer to inform a family member — usually a male — about the patient's condition. Doctors think a wife or other female family member will freak out on hearing such news.

Sure enough, at this place, too, the doctors tried to cover up the fact that my husband had cancer. When the doctor asked if we had a son, we started to suspect my husband was gravely ill. When we told them we didn't have children, they just withheld the information about my husband's condition.

Well, my husband and I weren't stupid. We realized what was happening and demanded that the doctor tell us directly what was wrong. So he started to speak in English using all kinds of terminology he thought we couldn't understand. And he mumbled, too. But we understood him. Plus, my husband could read his own chart, despite the doctor's poor handwriting.

We both decided it was probably wise to get a second opinion regarding his condition, so we headed over to the university hospital. My husband asked the doctors there to tell him flat out what the problem was. They diagnosed him with cancer in its early stage. So my husband underwent surgery and chemotherapy and recovered. Life was difficult for me afterward. The doctors prepared a list of things he could and couldn't eat, and I had to carefully consider the list every time I cooked. Too much meat is bad for the body. Lots of vegetables are good. Things like that. Then my husband did a self-diagnosis and determined the cancer would leave his body more quickly if I gave him an hour-long massage every day. I remember I was massaging him even while I was pregnant, my big belly bumping into the table. The massages continued for three years. It was hard work, but I guess I didn't mind too much. To me love is not saying something is a bother.

Four years into our marriage, we had a son, Shuichi. After the baby was born, my husband and I started sleeping in separate rooms. That's not too unusual here in this country. In fact, some women continue to share a room with the child until he reaches three or four years old. So, if a woman gives birth to three children, one right after the other, she might be sleeping apart from her husband for ten years.

I didn't mind sharing a room with my child instead of my husband. Actually, I preferred it. It was easier that way. My husband didn't want the baby's crying to wake him up in the middle of the night. And I was relieved to roll over in peace knowing I wasn't going to disturb my husband. Plus, I think I was going through postpartum. In Japan we call it "maternity blues." It's a hormonal reaction. It's also a cultural reaction. Here in Japan we say men go through it, too. Men are used to their wives mothering them, but after the birth of the baby, the wife is usually preoccupied with taking care of the newborn and doesn't have time for the husband. So he gets depressed. And then some women don't like to have sex after the baby is born. That causes other problems. We joke here about how men become more like sons to their wives than husbands. Some women refer to their husband as their firstborn son, and their male baby as their second son.

I did what I could to be a good mother, but sometimes it was difficult. The teachers at Shuichi's school used to send home letters encouraging the mothers to pack nutritious lunches for their children, things with lots of colors in them. Well, Shuichi doesn't like vegetables. He won't touch them. So his lunches were really dull looking. They were so brown. I eventually started buying colorful plastic vegetables and placing them in his lunch box just for show.

And the kids also had to have homemade *zōkin* [cleaning cloth]. I couldn't just give him an old T-shirt or towel from around the house to use during cleaning time at school. Instead I had to sew one for him. The teachers wanted us to sew cute little animals and designs on them. *She rolled her eyes.* Well, I didn't have time to do that, so my mother ended up sewing him a few.

Another thing we had to do as mothers was help the kids cross the street in the morning. I remember I was working at the time and tried to explain this to the administration at the school, but I couldn't get out of this duty. So I had to go in late to work. What I couldn't understand, though, was that in the afternoon the kids walked home alone, crossing the streets by themselves. What made the afternoon any safer than the morning? The afternoon is probably *more* dangerous since there are lots of people driving home from work tired.

I remember envying a friend of mine at the time who was married to a doctor. I thought she was lucky because she didn't have to work and could concentrate her energy on her housework and her children. But much more was expected of her because she didn't have an outside job. It went without saying that she'd devote every minute of the day to her household duties. Well, like anybody, she needed to get out of the house on occasion. In fact, she even talked about working part-time at McDonald's. So finally she asked her husband if she could get a job. Do you know what he said? He told her she could take an outside job as long as she made the same amount of money as he. But he's a doctor! How could she possibly make that much? The last I heard, she had a breakdown. As far as I know, she hasn't recovered.

I guess it was about five years into our marriage when my husband and I started having problems. I'd stopped doing things I knew he wanted me to do, and he seemed to stop caring. On top of that, little things started getting on our nerves. For example, my husband had an obsessive attitude toward his schedule. It was as if his personal schedule was the most important thing in the world! For instance, he went to bed at ten o'clock each night and made it a point to get eight hours of sleep. Well, some nights he couldn't sleep, so he just lay there irritated. Then around midnight he'd get up in a huff and re-set the alarm clock for eight o'clock, just to make sure he got those eight hours in. And, as luck would have it, the next morning around seven the phone would ring and wake him up. Then he'd stew the entire day over not getting eight hours of sleep.

Also, my husband didn't have a driver's license, so I had to drop him off at work each day. He used to make me wait around in the morning for the exact moment he was ready to leave for school. He never told me what his schedule was like, so I had to watch him and wait for an indication that he was ready to go. When I eventually went back to work, I didn't have time to drive him to the university, so he had to take a cab. We didn't even need to tell the taxi drivers where to come in the morning; they knew our place by heart.

Despite all of these little things, I never regretted marrying him; after all, we had a son together, and we *did* enjoy each other's company for a long time. I guess we just got tired of being with one another. You know, I thought marriage was going to be something like a dream, but it's a reality. When I got married I didn't know that. Now I do. It was a good lesson. Too many people think marriage is just something to do. Something they have to do. That's wrong. It's just another societal system.

What I do regret about my first marriage is that I didn't tell my husband I needed more warmth and passion in our relationship. I should've just spoken with him about how dissatisfied I was. Instead, I started having an affair. I made excuses to myself about needing to be loved, hugged, and spoiled by a man, and since I wasn't getting that at home, I was going to find it elsewhere. That was wrong. I know that now.

During the last five years of my marriage I had three affairs. The first man was a Japanese radio announcer whom I'd met at a previous job. I ran into him in Naha one afternoon while I was shopping, and we went out for a drink. That's when he told me how much he liked me. Shortly afterward I found myself leaving my baby with my mother and meeting him on different occasions. My husband never found out. I never felt guilty either. Like I said, to me marriage was just a system.

Then I started having an affair with a man in the U.S. Air Force. I was 28 years old at the time. He was really in love with me. When he eventually got transferred to mainland Japan he stayed celibate, thinking I'd get a divorce and go to the mainland to be with him. Well, after four years I just couldn't do it and ended up breaking it off with him. I'm ashamed at how I acted. I'm sure he must've hated me for that.

Then I met a marine. He was 20 years old. I was 32. I don't know what I was doing with him. Actually, yes I do. I think I was tired of being with people like my husband, who was really intelligent — too intelligent almost — and then with the air force guy who was quite serious himself. I just wanted a change. And I think in a way I wanted to retrieve my youth. I needed to feel young again. This is going to sound terrible, but that 20-year-old marine was so stupid. And in a weird way, that was what was so refreshing about our relationship. He was unlike anyone I'd ever been with. I remember buying him everything he wanted. I even paid for trips we took together. I was making forty-two hundred dollars a month as salary on base, and when I eventually broke up with him, I discovered I hadn't saved a penny. Not a cent. Every time he said he wanted something, I bought it for him. Once he mentioned seeing a beautiful 30-inch TV set that he couldn't afford. "How much is it?" I asked him. "Seventeen hundred dollars," he answered. "Oh, that's cheap," I told him, and bought it for him. I guess we used each other for different reasons.

Eventually he went home to the States and asked me to visit him that summer. I agreed and reserved a ticket to go to California in July. Then Ken, my present husband, called me up. He and I were friends at the time since we worked together at one of the city offices. Well, Ken's wife had just told him she wanted a divorce. Naturally he was upset. I remember we talked for a long time on the phone that night. Then, about a month or so later, Ken and I met to talk in person. That's when he confessed he liked me! Well, I told him I considered him just a friend and, besides that, I was involved with someone else at the time: the marine who'd just returned to the States. In fact, I was driving that marine's car. Ken noticed the Y license plate [3] and was surprised. I guess he realized at that point how serious I was about the marine.

I went about making my plans to go to the States, and when I told Ken about my trip, he said he thought I was making a big mistake. Well, I was set on going to California and told him so. Then, a few weeks later, Ken gave me a present: a guidebook to California. That's when I realized he was a fair person. That gesture meant a lot to me. So I called him up, and, well, we started dating. *She smiled.* My marine boyfriend wasn't so happy when I told him I wasn't going to visit him in California anymore. He'd already requested a month's vacation time to spend with me there.

In 1994 I filed for divorce. It's not too hard to get a divorce in Japan since it only involves signing some paperwork and sending it in. And, it doesn't cost anything like it does in the States. Generally a husband and wife split things fifty-fifty when they divorce, but in our case I didn't want a thing. I let him have all of the furniture and everything else. I guess I blamed myself for the way things turned out. I even gave him custody of our son. Like I said, my husband was a lot older than I, and I figured I might have a chance at getting remarried and having a second child, while our son was probably his last. Actually I did remarry shortly after all of this. Ken and I have been married now for four years. And even though my first husband has custody of our son, Shuichi still spends every other month with Ken and me.

Mariko-san paused for a moment.

When I look back on my relationships with the opposite sex over the years, I realize I've had a lot more relationships with American men here than with Okinawan men. I don't think that's unusual for women in this society. Lots of them prefer to date foreigners, not Japanese. In my opinion, the women in Okinawa who are attracted to American men are the ultra-independent females in this society. They're the ones who don't like the social system here, the one that mandates that women and men have to act a certain way in different social situations. Basically these women are independent thinkers.

I think Japanese guys are threatened by these independent women. Japanese men are attracted to females who conform, who play the cutesy game and act dumb. And they love women in uniforms. By the way, have you heard of *enjokōsai*? It's prevalent in Japanese society. Older — and I mean considerably older — Japanese men pay young high school girls in sailor-suit school uniforms to have sex with them. Abnormal, huh? But so many men do it. Why don't they target someone their own age? I wonder. This indicates there's something seriously wrong in our society. Men here are really turned on by young teens and by women like nurses who wear white uniforms. I swear it's a national preference among Japanese men to be attracted to these kinds of women. In the United States, nurses are respected, aren't they? I mean, they're seen as intelligent individuals. But here they're perceived as nothing more than angels, pure women in white dresses. They aren't looked upon as professionals. The same thing goes for stewardesses. So if men are attracted to these kinds of women, the independent females in our society who don't conform to these models seek out American men.

A lot of Okinawan women who date Americans have a preference for a certain race of American men. For example, some hang out at bars that cater to mainly whites, and others go to places that attract black clientele. The girls who are looking to date American military guys are usually young high school girls, so rather than focusing on a guy's personality or something, they tend to look at more superficial things such as if he's a good dancer, if he wears nice clothes, or if he has cool stereo equipment or something in his car.

Personally I never had a preference for black guys over white guys, or Hispanics over Asian-Americans. It didn't matter to me what race a man was. All I was concerned about was whether or not he was a gentleman. If he wasn't, I didn't want to date him.

I think one of the biggest differences between American men and Japanese men is the level of confidence they possess when it comes to dealing with the opposite sex. American guys approach women directly. And most women appreciate that, I think. But these men have to realize that some Okinawan women see them as nothing more than toys or playthings. Many don't expect to cultivate a serious relationship with someone in the military when they know he'll be leaving in a year. I think it's fair to say there are women who view the American men as playthings and the Japanese men as the ones to marry. I don't have statistics to confirm that, but I know it from talking with a lot of people.

Mariko-san concluded our discussion with her feelings about the U.S. military bases on the island.

As you know, the bases are a big part of Okinawa. I think everyone on the island realizes this. Personally, I don't feel exploited that they exist here. I guess I accept them as a matter of course. In fact, I think the average person here on the island doesn't think much about the existence of the bases. *She pointed to the insurance company across the street.* Do you think the people at that company over there really care if the bases are here or not? I don't think so. Unless they had a huge contract or something with the bases. There are people on the island, though, who are really concerned about the military presence here and devote their lives to seeing the facilities removed. But those people are few in number. Most average Okinawans don't seem to concern themselves with deep issues. They're worried about too many other things, such as providing food for their families.

Do I feel the bases should be withdrawn from the island? Well, Okinawa would be in a serious economic predicament if the bases weren't here. I mean, I think Okinawans are too optimistic about their ability to sustain the economy without the bases. A lot of Okinawans fear what would happen if the bases disappeared. Of course, most of them won't admit it since it's not politically correct to say things like that. If you live in Okinawa, you have to say you're anti-base. What really bothers me is that these anti-base people say *they're* the ones who are anti-war. Well, isn't everyone anti-war? I mean, can anyone say he's for war? I don't think so.

You'll also hear lots of people say things like they're bothered by the noise the military aircraft make. Personally, I think how much someone is affected by a certain noise depends on who makes the noise. Like I mentioned before, lots of people here blame the military for everything. If a person is anti-base, he's going to find some noise from the bases that bothers him. Now that I think about it, the *sakanaya-san* [fishmonger] makes more noise than the military aircraft do when he drives around in the morning screaming into his megaphone! So it's not fair to criticize only the bases for making a racket here.

Anytime something bad happens on Okinawa, people blame it on the bases and the military. Gradually the U.S. bases have become scapegoats for everything unfortunate that occurs in our society. Take, for example, the issue of traffic. The streets in Okinawa are like those in Bangkok, aren't they? Often it's quicker to reach a destination by bicycle than by car. Well, up north where there are a lot of bases, there's a lot of traffic. People have complained about this and blamed the traffic on the number of military personnel driving cars. Some people suggested developing a more sophisticated system of transportation on the island, such as a rail system, that might take care of this problem. The government won't construct a train system, though, since this would put the bus drivers out of work. Who would take the bus if there were trains? So the situation remains the same. It's almost as if people enjoy complaining about the fact that the bases are here. It takes the blame off the government and makes the problem seem like one that comes from outside society, not from within.

I have to admit that my remarks might be biased because I work on base. It's probably easy to be brainwashed by working there. For example, every morning and afternoon the American flag is raised and lowered, and people are expected to stand at attention while that's occurring. Sometimes I'm not there when it happens, but if I am, I stand at attention. And in the office where I work, there are pictures of the President of the United States and high military officials hanging on the wall. Those sorts of things remind me that I work on a U.S. base and probably shouldn't criticize the American presence here. But, I try not to be influenced by such things. I mean, I could easily be affected the opposite way by reading the local newspapers here, which are critical of the bases.

Even though a lot of Okinawans complain about the existence of the bases, many of them want to work there. Conditions are better on base than in Japanese companies. The salary is higher for one, and women aren't discriminated against. Some women here don't realize how much Japanese society discriminates against them until they come to work on base. Then they learn that they don't have to pour tea or prepare coffee for their fellow employees. Some women like to do those things, though. And if it makes them feel good to do that and to make others happy, then I can't criticize them. After all, can we generalize about what happiness is for people? I think it's a subjective thing.

I reflect a lot on what makes me happy. In other words, what it is about life that satisfies me. I like to learn, which is why I'm going to college now. I take classes at the University of Maryland campus on base. I'm working on a degree in psychology. I guess I wasted a lot of time in the past. *She smiled dryly.* Now I'm trying to catch up. At the rate I'm going, it may take as many as six years to get my bachelor's degree, but I'm going to complete it.

Thankfully, I'm satisfied with my personal life. I have a wonderful marriage and a terrific husband. Ken is a kind and understanding person who treats my son well. That's important to me. I have everything I want from my marriage: companionship as well as economic and emotional support.

I only hope my son can discover the same things in life. I want him to find someone who makes him happy the way my husband has made me happy. That's such an important thing. Also, I want my son to know that his father is a good person. So am I. It's just that things didn't work out between us when we were married. I'd like to apologize to my son for this in the future. I want to tell him I'm sorry his father and I had to divorce.

Who knows where we'll be in the future? Ken, Shuichi, and I may find ourselves in America someday. My husband would like to be a professor, so we might go to the States so he can get his Ph.D. If he did find a job at a university, I'd probably work as a freelance translator or something. My husband says I don't have to work; I can be dependent on him. But I want to work. And I think I could be happy working anywhere. As long as we're together, I can be happy anywhere.

8 : MAYUMI TENGAN

The north entrance of Ryukyu University is an area crowded with lun-
cheonettes, vending machines, photo shops, and Laundromats. On hot
afternoons the region buzzes with the chatter of college kids who stand
around smoking cigarettes between classes, their conversations regu-
larly disrupted by the roar of motorbikes and the burp of city buses. Stu-
dents on bicycles mingle with the motorists, pedaling down the street in
the wake of thick, black vehicular exhaust, its oily smell competing with
the aroma of fried pork cutlet from the nearby bentō *shop.*

Not far from the university's north gate is the 24-hour Hot Spar
convenience store. In the evenings the illuminated parking lot is filled
with rough-looking high school boys sporting copper-colored hairdos and
tribes of high school girls dressed in pleated uniform skirts, most hiked
up dangerously high at the waist. They flirt playfully with one another
and converse casually, the girls' high-pitched giggles piercing the quiet
night air. Above the convenience store is a six-story, concrete apartment
complex. This is where Mayumi Tengan, a 29-year-old graduate stu-
dent, lives with her husband and 5-year-old daughter.

Her appearance is stunning: onyx-colored eyes, long, raven-black
hair, and a broad, infectious smile, two deep dimples parenthetically
containing her wide grin. Mayumi-san is working toward her master's
degree at Ryukyu University. She is majoring in political science with
a concentration in women's studies and military issues. During our in-
terviews at her apartment, she discussed what it was like growing up in
Naha, the capital of Okinawa, during the 1980s, including the contact
she had with American servicemen at the time. She talked about how

her impressions of American military personnel as a young girl differed from her feelings about them as an adult, and why. In addition, Mayumi-san shared her reasons for founding Young Voice, an all-female organization designed to raise awareness among young women toward issues facing them in present-day Okinawan society, namely problems associated with politics, the military, and women's rights.

When I was a junior high school student in the early eighties, my dream was to have a baby that was half Okinawan and half American! I thought those biracial kids were so cute. You see, I was a big Phoebe Cates fan at the time. She's half Chinese and half American, isn't she? Anyhow, that's what I wanted to do with my life. When I told my mother about this, she just laughed. I guess she figured it was normal for a young girl to have such dreams.

Growing up here on Okinawa was a wonderful experience. It was unique to live in an environment surrounded by so many foreigners. As a child I remember thinking Americans were the greatest, that I was privileged to be from a place where so many of them resided. I guess I never really thought of the Americans here as military personnel, but rather just as ordinary American people. I mean, I never saw them wearing their military uniforms or anything. They were always in T-shirts and jeans. Maybe if I'd seen them running around in fatigues and carrying weapons I would've felt differently about them.

The first time I ever dated an American was when I was in high school. I met him at the McDonald's on *Kokusai Dōri* [International Street] in Naha. That area of the city was always swarming with military guys who looked like Tom Cruise. *She laughed.* Honestly, I couldn't distinguish one American from the other. I felt like I was on the set of a movie. I used to imagine all of these men were romantics, just like the ones in love scenes from American films. Silly, huh?

Anyhow, I was shopping downtown in Naha the day I met him. When I stopped off at McDonald's to get something to eat, I saw a girlfriend of mine sitting at a table inside with her military boyfriend and his friend. She introduced me to the friend, and we talked for a while. I remember I didn't speak English well at the time, so I had to communicate with him using gestures. Must've looked pretty funny! I think we hung out at McDonald's for an hour or so before we decided to go to a music bar down the street for a drink. The guy I was with ordered a beer for himself and a Coke for me since I was only

16 at the time. He was 20. What I remember most about him is that he had the coolest boots. They weren't cowboy boots, just sharp brown leather ones. Not many people on Okinawa wear boots because it's too warm here. But that guy wore them all the time. I think he was with the marines. Wait, maybe it was the air force. I don't remember. In any case, they all seemed the same to me.

When he asked me if I wanted to go out again sometime, I jumped at the chance. So, a few weeks later, he took me to see a movie on base. What an experience that was! Did you know that before the movie starts you have to stand up for the United States National Anthem? Really, there's a video that accompanies the music and everything. I loved standing while that song played because it made me feel like I was in America. I thought, "Wow, this is American culture!"

Before I knew it, I'd fallen head over heels in love with that marine. I guess we dated for about eight months, right until he was scheduled to go back to the States. Then, one month before he was supposed to leave, he called me on the phone to tell me he was going and that I should find a new boyfriend! Can you believe that? I was so hurt. I didn't see that coming at all. I moped around for a while until one of his friends called me up and asked me out. *She blushed.* That guy was really nice to me in the beginning, but then he went back to the States for one month during the summer, and when he returned to the island he stopped calling me. I found out from a friend of his that he was married. He used to take out his wallet and show me pictures of a child he referred to as his nephew. It was his son! I was so angry that he lied to me. I confronted him about this and, of course, he denied everything. "What are you talking about?" he shouted at me. "Are you gonna believe what my friends tell you, or what I tell you?" he asked. Well, I wanted to trust him, but I still felt deep down inside that he wasn't telling me the truth. After a lot of breakups and makeups I finally got tired of him and left. I guess he went back to the States for good.

I never dated any more military guys after that. But my reputation suffered enough from those two experiences alone. Word had gotten around at my high school that I was easy. A lot of girls even called me a bitch. Some of them were just jealous because they wanted to date a military guy. *She forced a smile.* Everywhere I went I got icy stares. Then rumors started that people had seen me kissing an American passionately in front of McDonald's or something like that. I'd never even held hands with my American boyfriends in public because I was afraid of that kind of talk! When my boyfriends asked me why I wouldn't hold hands in public, I used to lie and say I was shy. The truth is I didn't want anyone seeing me in public with an American and then spreading gossip about me. They did anyhow, though.

After I graduated from high school, I went to college here on the island. I wasn't excited to go to a university so close to home, but I didn't get into any of the colleges on the mainland to which I'd applied. My parents were the ones who made me send in an application to the national university here just in case I couldn't get in anywhere else.

I met a nice Okinawan guy during my first year at college, but I was afraid to date him. See, most of the students at this school were locals, and I thought maybe he'd already heard about my bad reputation from someone. It turns out he had, but he didn't care. We dated for a few years before I transferred to a university on the mainland. I wanted to change my major from English literature to psychology, and since we can't switch from one academic program to another at universities here, I had to transfer schools. I couldn't wait to go to the mainland to study. I wanted to get away from my parents and be independent for a while.

I loved going to school on the mainland. One of the funniest things about being an Okinawan up in Ehime Prefecture,[1] were the sorts of questions fellow students used to ask me about life on Okinawa. "Do you guys wear shoes down there?" or, "Is everyone fluent in English because of the military presence?" I used to laugh it off. It just goes to show you how little people know about our island. When Japanese mainlanders met me for the first time, they thought I was a Thai or a Filipina because I was dark from the sun. When I announced I'm Okinawan, they looked at me differently. "Oh, Okinawan," they repeated slowly. Then they didn't know what to say after that. Talk about feeling unique! I guess my sense of identity was strengthened up on the mainland. I became a lot more conscious of what it means to be Okinawan when I was surrounded by people who were different from me. I never got angry when the mainlanders asked me all types of strange questions about Okinawa because I didn't think they were being malicious; they were just curious.

Anyhow, during my senior year in college I found a job in Tokyo and was planning on going there after graduation to work. My boyfriend — the same guy I met at the university on Okinawa — had recently left for Australia on a working holiday visa. Well, when I went up to Tokyo for job orientation I got really ill, so sick I went to see a doctor. That's when I discovered I was pregnant. I couldn't believe it! And I had no way of getting in touch with my boyfriend in Australia since he'd just left and didn't have an address yet. The doctor told me I wasn't well enough to go back to Okinawa and that I had to stay there in Tokyo. So I stayed with my boyfriend's sister and her husband. Then I had to call my parents and explain everything. They weren't angry at all. As for my boyfriend, he was thrilled when he heard the news. You see, he ended up calling his sister's place a few days after I'd arrived there, and I told him over the phone that we were expecting a baby. He came home from Australia right away. I have to admit I was pretty scared and confused about the whole thing.

I didn't drop out of school, though. I attended classes while I was pregnant since I wanted to finish my degree. I don't know how many people even realized I was pregnant. My friends knew, of course, but since I was pregnant during the winter months, I was able to hide my belly with layers of clothing. I was never that big, so it wasn't very hard. What I remember most about my pregnancy is that it was a real chore. I was always sick and could hardly eat a thing. In fact, I think I was fatter after the baby was born than during my pregnancy because I started eating so much out of boredom after my daughter was born.

Shortly after I graduated from college, my husband and I got married. We didn't have a wedding ceremony; we just signed papers at the town hall. Our parents acted as witnesses. You know, I don't think I ever gave much thought to getting married. In fact, I guess in the back of my mind I always thought I'd stay single. Of course I wanted to wear a pretty white wedding dress once in my lifetime, but I didn't want a big party and ceremony and everything. Sometimes I fantasize about having a church wedding now since I didn't have one when I was younger. I don't know if I'll ever do it, but I think about it from time to time.

Once we were married, my husband and I rented an apartment together in Ginowan [a city in central Okinawa]. Then he went back to school to get licensed as a high school English teacher. I remember we were miserably poor at the time. I didn't have a car, so I had to ride the bus all the way up to Okinawa City where I was working as a tutor. My husband was employed part-time at night for a *juku* [cram school] and went to school during the daytime. He had some scholarship money, but we still had to pay part of the tuition and then, of course, rent and food. Our parents had to help us out financially in the beginning.

I don't know how to describe my marriage exactly. I mean, when my husband and I were newlyweds, we tried to do things together like go to the movies or out to dinner. We were always coordinating our schedules. These days we almost never do that. I guess the two of us go out about once a year. That's usually on our wedding anniversary in March. Every now and then we try to do things as a family, such as eat at a restaurant or something. But, to

CONTEMPORARY OKINAWAN WOMEN

tell you the truth, going out is a bit of a bother. When we do go somewhere as a family, my favorite thing to do is head to the beach in the summertime to fish or to swim.

Back when I was single I thought married life was supposed to be like the life my parents had together. My father was a university English professor, so he had a lot of time in the summer and on the weekends to do things with my mother, my two sisters, and me. I guess that's why I always dreamed of marrying a teacher; I wanted someone to do things with me and my daughter like my father did for our family. I married a teacher, but my husband's a busy man. He's a high school English instructor and the school baseball coach. He leaves home around 7:00 A.M. and usually doesn't return until 9:00 P.M. We don't even eat dinner together since he usually just grabs a bite to eat at school.

I used to think if a family didn't eat dinner together, or go out on the weekends together, they weren't a happy family. After all, that's the way I was raised. What I remember most about our family outings as a kid was going to the movies. We never went to see Japanese movies, just American ones. There were Japanese subtitles on the screen, so we could follow what was happening. The films I remember the most are *The Sound of Music, West Side Story,* and *The Exorcist.* Have you seen *The Exorcist?* Gosh, that was so scary!

We used to go out to dinner a lot, too. I never heard my father complain once about eating out. Some men would've made a fuss if their wives decided not to cook but to eat at a restaurant instead. He didn't say a word, though. I wouldn't call my father easy-going or anything. In fact, he was the strict one of the two. But he didn't get angry over things like that.

Our favorite place to eat was Pizza House. At that time there was only one Pizza House on the island, and it was located in Ginowan. I think it's still there, but it's more like a fast-food place these days. When I was little, though, it was a nice restaurant. Almost everyone who went there was American. I used to think only Americans could eat there and that my family had just gotten in somehow by chance. Even the hostess who sat us was American.

My mother knew this particular restaurant well because she used to go there with friends from the bank back in the days when she worked. I don't know how to describe my mother exactly. I guess I'd call her unconventional. What I mean is, she wasn't a typical Japanese mother who tried to do everything by the book. She didn't even get married until she was 30! My father was 32. They only dated for four months. I think their relatives and friends were badgering them to get married because they were both getting older. So my mother quit her job at the bank, got married, and had children. I don't know if she ever regretted it. I never asked her.

I think she regretted not being able to go to college, though. See, her parents were conservative and didn't think girls needed to get a university education. So my mother worked full time after she graduated from high school until she married my father. She used to tell me stories about how she made her own money and bought nice things for herself. I always thought she was lying to me. I mean, my mother never seemed like a person with power; all she did at home was listen to my father. I never wanted to be like her when I was a child; I wanted to be someone a bit more independent. In fact, as a kid I used to get angry at her because she was always at home. Most of my friends' mothers had jobs, so they got to walk home with their own house keys and unlock the doors and do whatever they wanted after school. I used to wish I was a latchkey kid, too. *She smiled.*

Looking back on my childhood, though, it was a happy one. Life was easy as a kid; not a thing to worry about. I remember my favorite time of the year was the *Obon* season.[2] That's when the relatives used to gather at my parents' home to celebrate. They always came to our place since that's where the *ihai* [ancestral tablets] are kept. My father is the oldest son in his family, so he's in charge of taking care of the *ihai*. He keeps them on the *butsudan* [Buddhist altar] in our living room. Before beginning the *Obon* meal, my father offered up the food to the ancestors. Things like thick slices of pork, *konbu* [kelp], *gobō* [burdock], *kamaboko* [fish paste], fish tempura, and sticky *mochi* [rice cake]. He placed a plate of food on the *butsudan,* then lit some incense and waited while the ancestors' spirits symbolically ate the food. My grandfather was strict and used to make us wait until the whole stick of incense burned out before we could eat. "The ancestors haven't finished eating yet!" he'd cry at us as we sat there listening to our stomachs growl and begging him to let us start the meal. Sometimes my mother let us sneak something to eat in the kitchen while we were waiting. If my grandmother or grandfather ever knew that, they'd have a fit.

What I remember vividly about the meal is that the women never ate with us. The male adults and children used to sit in the living room watching TV and talking while the women congregated in the kitchen preparing the food. When it was ready, they served it to us, then scurried back to the kitchen where they stood around and ate their meal. Unfair, huh? I always thought it was. Especially when I was in junior high school and had to start helping them! The women always acted like they didn't mind eating in the kitchen. "There's not enough room out there for everyone to sit," they used to say. I guess it was then when I realized what a burden the holiday season was on my mother.

Around the end of April there's another religious holiday that people here on the island celebrate. It's called *seimei*. At this time, relatives gather at the family grave to pray to the ancestors. It's sort of like a big picnic. We offer flowers, *ocha* [green tea], and incense to our ancestors and then, just like *Obon*, we place the food we're going to eat that day on the altar as a sign of respect to them. After that, we pass it around and eat it. *Seimei* might seem a lot like *Obon*, but it's different because at *Obon* time the deceased souls visit our houses, whereas at *seimei* time, we visit their graves. I remember this holiday was hard on my mother, too, since she was responsible for preparing all the food by herself. See, as the wife of a firstborn son, she was in charge of making all of the traditional Okinawan foods, enough to feed the dozens of relatives who gathered at our family's graveside that afternoon. That was quite a task for a person like my mother who doesn't even like to cook! Before she got married I don't think she ever prepared a meal by herself at home. Her mother spoiled her, I heard. That's why my mother was happy when stores on the island started preparing the *jūbako* [nest of boxes that hold festival foods] filled with traditional foods about ten years ago. Now she just buys the entire meal at the grocery store instead of laboring for hours in the kitchen.

I guess the best holiday as a child, though, was New Year's Day. That's when we got *otoshidama* [small gifts of money from relatives and friends who come to the home to visit]. My sisters and I used to make tons of money. Everyone who visited our house slipped us a small envelope as they came in. When I was an elementary school student I used to receive about 500 yen [four dollars][3] per envelope. Once I reached junior high school age it jumped to 1000 yen [eight dollars]. Then as a high school student I received 2000 yen [sixteen dollars]. Of course my grandparents always gave us a little more than distant relatives, sometimes as much as 5000 yen [forty dollars]. When I was little I used to hand over the money to my mother for safekeeping. She always put it into the bank for me. Then when I was in high school I got to keep it and do whatever I wanted to with it. I used to buy things like clothes or books or movie tickets.

The doorbell rang, and she excused herself to answer it. The caller was a salesman peddling books. Mayumi-san spoke politely with the man for several moments before returning to her place at the kitchen table. Then she continued our conversation, this time focusing on her current involvement in women's issues and what inspired her to create the organization, Young Voice.

I first got interested in issues related to Asian women when I started working at Seminar House[4] three years ago. At that time I heard about a trip to the Philippines to visit a support center there for women. In the days before Subic Bay[5] was closed, the Filipina women who worked in industries surrounding the base used to drop their children off at the support center where they were cared for until the mothers finished working. After Subic closed, the women lost their jobs. So the support center was converted into a place to teach these women skills such as sewing. But the women there couldn't afford more than a few sewing machines. That's when we started sending over machines for them to practice on. All of the machines were donated from Okinawan citizens. Unfortunately the equipment wasn't making it to the destination, so we decided to deliver it personally. Ten of us from Seminar House went on one particular trip, each of us toting a sewing machine as carry-on luggage. We also brought scissors, thread, cloth, and other supplies for the women.

My trip to the support center piqued my interest in the Philippines. And in Okinawa there are plenty of opportunities to study about the Philippines given the number of Filipina women who work on the island as dancers in bars that cater to GIs. When I got back to Okinawa, I decided to go to one of the bars where the Filipina women work. There weren't many people there that night, so the girls approached me after they finished talking with their customers. I think they were excited to speak with an Okinawan woman since the only contact they had at the bar was with drunken American guys. They asked me if I'd come back and visit them. They lived in an apartment above the bar. I went to visit a few times and gradually developed a friendship with them. We usually talked about the Philippines or customs in Okinawa. I never went over there to try and talk the women out of working at the bars as dancers or anything. And I didn't discuss religious or moral issues either.

Most of these Filipina women come to Okinawa to work in order to raise money for their families back home. Others come in the hope of marrying an American or a Japanese. Some do. And some of those relationships work while others fail. It's sad, but a lot of the girls who come here for the first time are misinformed about the type of "entertaining" they're expected to do. Quite a few of them have been trained in ballet back home, and come over here thinking they're going to be professional dancers. Instead, they end up working in go-go bars and dancing in their bras and panties for the GIs. There are some women, though, who are here for a second or third time. They're the ones who know exactly what they're doing. Not all of the girls are naive.

I really wanted to continue learning about Asian women and the problems females all over Asia face these days, not just in Okinawa. So I decided to go to the 1995 NGO [nongovernmental organization] Forum on Women held in Peking, China. I talked with the staff at Seminar House who were sending a delegation to China, and they told me I could accompany them if I got involved in one of the workshops they were forming in anticipation of the conference. One of the women I knew from Seminar House was involved in issues related to military violence and women in Okinawa, so I decided to join her group.

It might seem funny that I'd get involved in research related to violence and the military considering my past experiences dating American GIs. I don't believe the military are bad people. I'm against the military as a structure, not its persons as individuals. Once I started researching the history of violence against women here, I discovered a lot about Okinawa that I didn't know before. I was coming across so many incidents of sexual and social violence committed by the U.S. military over the years. Prior to this I thought the bases were great. I think I was confusing the military culture with American culture, and that's a mistake because they aren't the same. The military culture is one based on violence since its members are trained to kill.

Interestingly, when I was doing this research prior to going to Peking, I couldn't find any statistics on the Japanese Self-Defense Forces (SDF)[6] and how many social crimes they've committed over the years. Surely they aren't completely innocent. The only information and statistics that exist concern the U.S. military. I know there must be information about the SDF, but both the police and the Okinawan Prefectural Government Office insist they have nothing. Maybe if I had the right connections I could get some information. You see, there are stats on the number of crimes committed by Japanese but they aren't broken down by job, so we don't know how many of these crimes are committed by SDF men. I think that's odd.

You know, I was hesitant at first to go to Peking because my daughter was young at the time. Just 2 years old. I was afraid when I went to her nursery school to tell the teacher I was going to be away in China for a few weeks and that my husband would be picking up our daughter after school, the teachers would judge me. "What kind of mother would leave a child under 3 years old to go off to a foreign country!" I could just hear them saying.

I brought this issue up at the conference in Peking and was relieved to hear a lot of women sympathize with me. Many of the American women there couldn't understand why people might judge a woman if she left her child with her husband and went off to do something for herself. They kept telling me I wasn't a bad mother; it was Japanese society that was at fault. I think they're right. Japanese society puts so much pressure on women to be good mothers. If you leave your child for a few hours to go someplace and relax, you're looked upon as an unfit mother. There were days when I wanted to drop my baby off with my mother or grandmother and go shopping or just do something for diversion, but I couldn't. People would talk. "These young mothers don't know how to take care of their children properly," they'd say. So, I did like I was supposed to do and never separated from my baby. The only time I got out of the house was when I went to the grocery store.

Naturally I was unhappy. I did nothing but eat sweets, partly out of boredom and partly out of frustration. I swear sometimes I thought about running away, just leaving my baby and my life behind and taking off. I can comprehend the mental anguish that drives some young mothers to commit suicide. The pressure placed on new mothers in this society is overwhelming.

Anyhow, it was good for me to be in Peking. It gave me the opportunity to network with other women from around the world and to find out what sorts of issues they have to deal with in their home societies. Do they have the same social problems as we do here in Japan? Are the demands placed on them the same demands that are placed on us Japanese women? Not many young women in Okinawa are concerned with the problems women face today, so I was excited to meet up with a bunch of enthusiastic women at the conference and to discuss serious topics with them. Fortunately there were three other Okinawan women in Peking around my same age. We talked quite a bit and agreed to keep in contact once we returned to Okinawa.[7]

When we got back here to the island, the four of us decided to form a group called Young Voice. It's a support group of sorts made up of young women between the ages of twenty and thirty. What we hope to do through this group is increase awareness among young people in contemporary Okinawan society about political, military, and social issues affecting us. The reason we decided to limit participation in the group to females is that we think girls act differently when men are around. Too many of them try to act cutesy. I think that's society's fault. In other words, if a girl doesn't act ladylike, she's criticized. So, in order to ensure that women speak up and express their opinions, and to be certain that they debate seriously about social issues, we limited participation in the group to females.

Young Voice deals with a variety of topics, not solely those concerning violence and the military. The issue of military violence is my specialty, but another woman is involved in topics related to the environment, while the other two original members specialize in labor and welfare problems. We meet monthly to discuss these and other political topics and to recommend solutions to them. We also work hard at networking and making women aware of the problems that we face in our society these days. I think that's important. I mean, the first step in solving problems is recognizing they exist.

I'm working on my master's degree right now. When I finish next year, I'd like to find a job on the island with a nongovernmental organization or a nonprofit organization. Ideally I'd like to work at a center for women where I can put my education and experience to use. What's important to me is being able to make my own money, enough to live on. I want to be financially independent. I don't need to be rich, though. I hope I never end up taking a job simply for the money. That's not what life is about in my opinion. I want to have a job that satisfies me, something that's worth getting up for in the morning.

What I want people here to understand is that the root of so many of our social problems on Okinawa is inequality between the sexes. Women need to be regarded as equal with men. Too often women are ignored, glossed over, taken for granted. People say Okinawan women are strong, but I don't know about that. They may voice their opinions, but many end up obeying their husbands in the end.

Also, I don't think we always see the problems people have in their marriages or relationships either; things are hidden well. And because people think women here are so strong, they don't think they could possibly be abused physically or psychologically. If a woman's a victim of physical abuse, she's usually encouraged by those around her not to say anything about it. That's wrong. It's a shame we don't have many support centers here to help out women like that. I'd like to see more of those kinds of places throughout the island. Actually, throughout all of Asia. I don't think Okinawan women are the only ones around the world dealing with these problems; I'm sure other Asian women have similar problems in their own countries.

Those are the dreams I have for myself. I also have aspirations for my daughter. I know as she grows she'll have her own, but there are certain things I want for her in my heart. I honestly hope she'll be her own person and not try to be someone that society tells her she has to be. I want her to develop an independent sense of self, a definition of who she is based on how she feels, not based on how society tells her she has to feel. I also want her to know she can do anything in life.

What worries me about her starting first grade next spring is that she's already influenced by peers at school. For example, one day I tried to put her in a pair of blue slacks, and she told me "girls don't wear blue; that's a boy's color." I asked her why she thought that. She told me that at school girls wear pink or red, and boys wear blue or green. Then she insisted girls should wear skirts and dresses, not pants. I was shocked to hear what she was saying. I sat her down and talked with her about this. I asked her about some of the teachers at school. "What was Mrs. So-and-So wearing today?" "Slacks," she answered. "Well, Mrs. So-and-So is a woman, isn't she?" My daughter agreed with me. "See, there's nothing wrong with wearing slacks if you're a woman. People wear them because they're comfortable," I reasoned with her. I think what happened was one of the kids at school told my daughter she looked like a boy. It was after that that she decided she wasn't going to wear pants anymore. Once I talked with her, I think she realized how silly it was to think that way. But, you know, she still prefers pink princessy dresses, despite our talk. *She chuckled.*

What scares me is how society can influence us, even a 4-year-old child, to think a certain way. Perhaps it's done unconsciously or unintentionally. But when things at school are always divided into two sections, girls and boys, it's only natural that children start to think and act in a particular way. I'm so afraid that my daughter is going to lose her sense of individuality once she starts elementary school. The educational system here has a way of conditioning people to conform.

In addition to the dreams I have for me and my daughter, I also have dreams for Okinawa. It's interesting, but up until I went to the Peking conference in 1995, I thought Okinawa was a pure place, a proud base-centered island. It was only after I started studying and learning more about the island and the role of the military here that my perception of the place changed. I started to realize that the bases here aren't a representation of America; the bases symbolize the military and, like I said, that's an entirely different culture.

I'm still surprised at how little I knew about the bases before I went to Peking. I mean, I never thought seriously about why they exist on the island, and what sort of problems they pose. I grew up in Naha where there weren't any bases, so it was easy to pretend that all of those military guys hanging out on *Kokusai Dōri* were just ordinary American civilians. But after I got married and moved to central Okinawa where most of the bases are concentrated, I became more conscious of the heavy military presence on the island. I could hear the helicopters roaring over my apartment complex every afternoon, and I could see how close some houses were situated to the wire fences surrounding the bases. Then, of course, the rape case occurred in 1995, convincing us more than ever that the U.S. military presence here means danger. All of these things made me realize that having the bases on the island isn't quite as cool as I once thought.

I'd like to see some things on the island change, beginning with the removal of the U.S. military bases, the Japanese bases, and the training grounds here. Of course this'll cause an economic crisis on the island since the Okinawan economy is still dependent on the U.S. bases for survival. That's why Okinawa needs to change its type of economy so it can exist independently of the bases. I think we can do that, but it isn't going to happen anytime soon. At least not until we're financially and psychologically free from that dependence. Okinawa is going to be OK in the end, though. We're going to survive.

9 : MAIKO SUNABE

Yomitan Village, located in north-central Okinawa, is well known for its fierce sense of tradition and unflagging pride. Villagers boast of their hometown's beauty, and triumph at the region's devotion to the arts, especially the art of pottery. In July 1997, residents of Yomitan had another reason to brag: one of their young women, 21-year-old Maiko Sunabe, was crowned Miss Okinawa.

Maiko-san is a beautiful young woman with shoulder-length sable-black hair and a charming dimpled grin. She resides in Yomitan Village with her father, mother, grandmother, older twin sisters, and younger brother. During our conversations, Maiko-san regaled me with anecdotes about growing up on Okinawa during the 1980s and 1990s, explaining why her childhood on the island was a unique one. She also shared with me her feelings about young people in Okinawan society today, and how both mainland Japanese and resident American military personnel have influenced the way in which Okinawan youth choose to express their identity and individuality. She also discussed her thoughts about her public position as Miss Okinawa and what she has learned through this job over the past year, including how it has strengthened her sense of identity as an Okinawan.

Yomitan, Maiko Sunabe's hometown, is a special place, a part of the island where antiwar sentiment is extreme, and where demonstrations against the vast American military presence are frequent. On April 1, 1945, American soldiers landed at nearby Sobe Beach and have occupied a large portion of this region ever since. Almost 50 percent of the land in Yomitan has been taken over by military installations, and much of the village's available housing is rented by American families.

Yomitan Village gained fame in 1987 when its most famous son, Shoichi Chibana, burned the Hinomaru, *the Japanese flag, at the National Athletic Meet held at Heiwa no Mori Ball Park. Many villagers supported Chibana's act, sharing his belief that the Rising Sun represents aggression and misery; in short, that it is symbolic of war. Considering Yomitan's torturous wartime history, this reaction seems natural.*

Perhaps the most visible reminder of the village's agonizing past is the Chibichirigama, *or Chibichiri Cave, where eighty-four Okinawans killed themselves, or were killed by their families, in a mass suicide during the early days of the Battle of Okinawa. Nestled low beneath the land at the bottom of a precarious dirt slope, the entrance to this cave is marked by a haunting statue of peace, the expressions on the stone skulls a mix of melancholy and madness. The statue was destroyed in 1987 by right-wing extremists in retaliation for Chibana's burning of the* Hinomaru. *It was restored eight years later in time for the fiftieth anniversary of the end of World War II. Even today, Chibichirigama's dark interior remains littered with the bones of the deceased, a chilling reminder of the victims' former presence and a sad symbol of their deplorable end.*

My conversations with Maiko-san took place in Yomitan. One cool February afternoon we met at a tea salon in the village, a chic, newly built place hidden down a gravel road off the main highway. The teahouse was sparsely populated when we entered, allowing us to secure a round table near the windows. High ceilings and French doors gave the interior a European flavor, while coral-colored tablecloths and white walls added a bit of fresh island color. Classical music echoed softly throughout the room. We ordered from the waiter and began our conversation.

I moved to Yomitan Village when I was in second grade. Before that my family was living in Okinawa City.[1] What I remember most about growing up in Yomitan is seeing dozens of American kids waiting outside for school buses to shuttle them to their schools inside the bases. They used to call out "Hello!" to my friends and me in English. We waved and said "Hello!" to them, too, but we weren't able to say anything else; that's all the English we knew.

My elementary school was located right next to an American military facility. There was a huge wire-mesh fence separating them from us. Since this area was very noisy, the windows at my school were double paned. And there was even an air conditioner in each classroom. We were allowed to turn it on when the weather got hot and we were forced to close the windows because of the noise. I always thought it was pretty cool to have an air conditioner in the classroom. After all, at my school in Okinawa City we only had a fan in the summertime.

You've seen the elephant cage,[2] right? It's that big, round, wire ring on the other side of town near my elementary school. Well, the U.S. military used to do their parachute drills near there. I remember looking out the classroom window one day and seeing a bunch of military guys parachuting down from the sky and landing near the fence. "What in the world's going on?" I wondered as I watched the men falling from the sky. After a while, though, it didn't shock me anymore; it became a normal sight. "Oh, there they go again!" I used to say to myself when I saw the parachutes.

The military usually did their parachute training on Mondays and Wednesdays, so the road heading toward my home was blocked off on those days for safety reasons. I think that was because a parachutist landed in the playground of my elementary school about twenty years ago, hurting a little girl. This was the same recess yard the tourists used to flock to with their big cameras to take pictures of the men behind the fences. Just like a circus attraction or something! The teachers at school were always reminding us not to go near the fence during recess time. "Stay away from the fence!" they'd warn us before we went outside to play.

I grew up surrounded by Americans, so I was never afraid of them like a lot of Okinawans are. I mean, there just didn't seem to be anything to fear. They always said hello and seemed friendly. Japanese people don't generally say hello when they see someone on the street, but the Americans always do. They're quick to shake hands and tell you their name. I like that.

In fact, I can't imagine what Okinawa would be like if the Americans weren't here. To me it's normal that the U.S. military bases are on the island. Maybe that's because I was born into this society and never experienced life here when the Americans weren't around. If the U.S. military left, I don't know what we'd do with all the empty bases, especially ones like Kadena that are so big. Older people on the island like my grandmother can imagine life without the bases, but that's because they remember Okinawa from the prewar period. They're always talking about a return to those days.

It's a shame, but I don't know much about prewar Okinawan society. Or about World War II. My grandparents told me a little bit about the war, but I didn't learn too much about it at school. In our textbooks, facts about World War II, such as where and when a certain incident took place, were reported, but there were never any details about those incidents. For example, I don't remember learning the particulars about crimes the Japanese military committed in Okinawa or throughout Asia.

At school, the only time the war gets discussed seriously is when Memorial Day rolls around each year on June 23.[3] Usually a week before this day, teachers show us a documentary film or something about the Battle of Okinawa and encourage us to ask our grandparents and parents about it at home. My grandmother was in Yokohama [on the Japanese mainland] during wartime, so naturally she couldn't tell me much about conditions here on Okinawa. And my grandfather wasn't on the island, either. He was stationed with the Japanese military somewhere on the mainland. At home he never talked about his war experiences. Every once in a while he said something like, "We were really poor during the war and didn't have much to eat, so be happy that you've got it so good!" Other than that, I didn't hear too much else about the past.

There's been some controversy recently over whether or not June 23 should be a national holiday on the island. I think it should be; if it weren't, people might start to forget about the past. At least by recognizing this day, Okinawans who experienced the war here are more likely to talk about what happened with their children and grandchildren. It's hard for young people like me who've never experienced war to understand the pain and sadness people of my grandmother's generation feel on this day, but I still think it's important not to forget what they went through.

One way some people on the island recognize Memorial Day is by visiting places like *Chibichirigama* or *Himeyuri-no-tō* [Cave of the Virgins].[4] These people are usually the ones who lost close relatives during the war. Fortunately my family didn't lose anyone in the war, so we don't go to those spots. Even though *Chibichirigama* is located right here in Yomitan, I've never been there. At least I don't think I've been there. Maybe I went when I was in elementary school or something. I've been to *Himeyuri-no-tō*, though, once when I was in junior high school, and then again when a friend from the mainland came here to visit.

I remember when I was a university student on the mainland and June 23 came around. No one up there even recognized it. Sometimes it wasn't even mentioned on the TV news. It seemed like the mainland Japanese didn't care about what was going on in Okinawa.

The mainlanders don't understand much about us, that's for sure. They have a lot of misconceptions and stereotypes about the Okinawans. For instance, when I was in Shimane Prefecture[5] a few months ago for my work as Miss Okinawa, a Japanese guy walking down the street called out to me in English, "Hello!" To be honest with you, that made me angry. It was as if Okinawa isn't even part of Japan. Like it's a foreign country or something. Do people on the mainland actually think we can't understand Japanese here? I didn't answer that guy when he called out to me in English; I just smiled and said nothing.

Other situations like that occurred when I was a college student in Tokyo. People up there thought of Okinawa as an independent island; its own little country. When they met an Okinawan they always said something like, "Oh, you're from Okinawa? Gee, I couldn't begin to understand that dialect you speak down there!" As if we all use the dialect here! I'm Okinawan and even *I* can't understand it.

And in the university dorms everyone thought I was a "half" [a child born of parents from two different races; in this case, Caucasian-American and Okinawan]. They used to ask me if my grandfather or some other relative was an American. When I explained that I'm Okinawan, people relaxed and said, "Oh, that's why you look half!" or something like that. They said my face resembled a foreigner's.

Even though people on the mainland don't know much about us islanders, for some reason they think it's cool to have a friend from Okinawa. For example, every time I went to a party or somewhere with my mainland friends, they introduced me as their friend, Maiko, from Okinawa. But when they introduced someone from elsewhere on the mainland such as Gunma,[6] they didn't say, "This is so-and-so from Gunma Prefecture." They just introduced that person by his name. So why the distinction for Okinawans? I hated that. It was like those people were just showing off that they had a friend from Okinawa.

In my position as Miss Okinawa, too, I've gotten a lot of strange attention from the mainland Japanese. A few months ago I had to go to Okayama Prefecture[7] for the Momotaro *Matsuri* [Momotaro Festival]. All of the regional Misses from Japan met up there for the festival and rode through the streets in open-top cars while people took pictures of us. Well, there was this one guy with a big camera who ran alongside my car the entire day. He wouldn't take pictures of anyone else — just me. He was carrying a big album filled with photos of former Misses. He kept trying to show me the album while he ran next to the car. He must've had a hundred photos in there! One of the former Miss Okinawas had warned me about the "Miss-mania" on the mainland, and people like that man who love to photograph the girls from Okinawa. She said the only thing you can do is try to ignore those kinds of people. Well, I tried, but it's hard to wave and smile at the crowd without smiling at him, too. We had to be friendly to everyone.

I was crowned Miss Okinawa last July. The pageant in Okinawa is a lot different from the Miss America pageant in the States. Here we have three winners, not just one. I don't know why they choose three girls. I guess it just means there aren't any runners-up; all three girls come in first. We each have a different title, though. For example, one girl is Miss Sky Blue, another is Miss Cobalt Blue, and I'm Miss Green-Green Gracious. The sky blue represents the Okinawan sky, the cobalt blue stands for the sea, and the gracious green symbolizes the flowers and greenery throughout the island.

Maiko-san reached for her purse and removed her wallet, opening it to pictures of her family and friends. Then she handed me a photo of her smiling modestly from a thronelike chair in the dressing room of the pageant hall. She was outfitted in a puffy white wedding dress with a scooped neck. A tall silver crown was perched precariously on her head.

All of the Miss Okinawa contestants had to wear wedding dresses. The pageant committee chose the gowns. They even picked out the swimsuits and the *yukata* [informal cotton summer kimono] that we wore. I remember we had to hurry and change outfits between the commercial breaks. There were people helping us, of course, but the whole situation was really frantic. I think they got that *yukata* on me in about three minutes! That's with the *obi*[8] and everything.

About ten years ago, the girls in the pageant had to model formal Japanese-style kimono and business suits that they picked out themselves. The judges wanted to see what sort of fashion sense the contestants had. Back then things were a lot more formal. Nowadays the pageant is relaxed and informal. I think there were some complaints from people in the past that the position of Miss Okinawa was nothing more than a decoration, something for show. So the committee changed the rules around a lot. Now the position is one of a tourism representative. There's less of an emphasis on looks and shapes.

I guess I've always been fascinated with the Miss Okinawa pageant. I used to watch it on TV every summer. Then, when I was in college in Tokyo, I started thinking seriously about trying out for it. My parents didn't pressure me or anything. In fact, when I mentioned I was thinking of sending in an application to participate in the contest, my father was embarrassed! He didn't think I'd make it. On the night of the pageant, my grandmother and mother came to the convention center to watch, but my father said he wasn't going to come. You know, though, he broke down and showed up at the pageant anyhow. He sneaked in quietly during the middle. *She giggled.*

Once I was selected as Miss Okinawa, I didn't really know what I was expected to do. I knew I was a representative for the prefecture, but I didn't know what that involved. I didn't realize I'd have the chance to travel to mainland Japan doing public relations work for Okinawa. This year I had the chance to go to places like Shimane Prefecture to promote Okinawan foods such as *goya* [a bitter, green root used in cooking] and *uchincha* [tea made from *ukon* root, a plant in the ginger family]. Then I went to Akita Prefecture[9] to celebrate the start of a direct flight from Akita to Okinawa. I even had the chance to go to Taiwan to promote tourism between our two islands. It was my first trip abroad!

My job as Miss Okinawa has been great. During the past year I enjoyed introducing Okinawan culture to people on the mainland. What I liked most was traveling to mainland Japan with a group of performers such as musicians and dancers because we got to teach everyone how to do folk dances from the island. People get into that. Sometimes we even play quiz games as a way of introducing the island to the mainland Japanese. We ask questions like, "What kind of animal skin do we use to make *sanshin?*" or, "What's the prefectural tree of Okinawa?"[10]

Whenever I'm on the mainland, I'm conscious of the fact that Okinawa is unique. We have a special dialect here, and our culture is unlike anything up there. I guess the one time I truly felt that Okinawa was different from the mainland was when I visited Kanazawa.[11] It's a beautiful place, filled with all sorts of cultural relics. What surprised me about Kanazawa, though, was that the people there never experienced war. When I asked them why their prefecture was spared during World War II, they told me it was because there are a lot of cultural artifacts there. When I heard that, I couldn't help but think about Shuri Castle in Okinawa and how it was destroyed during wartime. Wasn't Shuri Castle a cultural relic, too? Is it less important than the ones on the mainland? I didn't ask that question, but I was thinking it. It made me feel sad. That's when I realized that Okinawa's history is so much different from that of the mainland.

Our discussion gradually shifted toward the topic of young people on the island today, and the issue of identity and self-expression among them.

Young people here aren't that different from the ones on the mainland. Most like to color their hair or wear things like baggy clothes or grunge clothes, just to be different. I think TV has a big influence on their styles. I don't necessarily think teenagers are trying to look American or anything. In fact, most of the people whose styles they like to copy are Japanese — female

Japanese actresses and models. Whenever young girls see a Japanese actress with a new hairstyle, they want to imitate that style. People don't seem to be satisfied if they think they look like everyone else.

Of course this comes in waves. At one point we're imitating a certain person, and at other times another. Namie Amuro [Okinawan teen idol] has been popular here recently. Girls are always trying to mimic her clothing, her makeup, and her hairstyle. We also try to copy some Westerners' hairstyles, especially those of supermodels like Claudia Schiffer. I like her a lot.

Sometimes the girls who date Americans try to imitate their styles, too. For example, girls who date black guys dress in hip-hop fashions. They're those baggy clothes that don't show body curves; they just hang on you. Lots of stores on Gate Two Street outside Kadena Air Base sell these kinds of clothes. I guess young people have lots of reasons for dressing this way. Some are influenced by the music, and others just do it because they like it. One of my female friends was dating a guy who wanted her to wear hip-hop styles because they cover a girl's curves. He said when she wore tight-fitting dresses she was attracting too much attention from other guys. "When you're dating someone, you shouldn't show all your curves to everyone else in the place," he told her.

I think young Okinawans start trying to look different from others when they're in junior high school or high school. In elementary school we wear whatever we want to class, but after that we have to wear uniforms. In junior high school, the uniforms were navy blue sailor-suit ones with a small necktie and a pleated skirt. *She picked up a pen and hastily sketched the uniform in my notebook.* Well, lots of girls tried to alter the appearance of their uniforms to stand out from the crowd. Ten years ago long skirts were popular, so most girls wore their uniform skirts down past their calves. The teachers didn't like that; they wanted the uniforms worn properly: the hem right at the calf. These days girls hike up their uniform skirts to show off their legs. Short skirts are in style now.

Other girls tried to get away with wearing colored socks instead of white ankle socks like we were supposed to wear. If the teachers caught them in colored socks, they confiscated the socks and made the girls go barefoot for the rest of the day. Other girls used to hem the top part of their uniform — the shell that covered the blouse — until it almost touched their breasts. Of course they usually got in trouble for this during uniform inspection time, which occurred about twice a month. Or was it twice a week? I forget.

Lots of kids rebelled in high school, too, just like junior high. For example, girls permed their hair or dyed it even though we weren't supposed to do that. I remember I even pierced my ears at the time. Unfortunately one day my teacher noticed and made me take the earrings out. I haven't opened them up again. *She pulled her long hair away from her face and showed me her earlobes.*

Most of my classmates and I started dating during high school. We didn't have cars,[12] so we went to places nearby, mainly clubs where Okinawans hung out, not Americans. It wasn't until after high school graduation that a lot of girls started dating American guys. There was more of a chance to meet them out in town then.

American guys are really different from Okinawan guys. I mean, what I think is cool about the Americans is that they believe in the policy of Ladies First. That's why you'll see so many Okinawan girls dating American men and hardly ever the opposite: Western women with Okinawan guys. In fact, I couldn't even imagine seeing an American woman with an Okinawan; he just wouldn't treat her the way she was probably used to being treated.

Also, Americans are quick to give you a hug, even if you're a stranger. I think that's a good thing. What's unusual about American guys, though, is they think if a girl's dancing by herself at a club that means she's lonely. How ridiculous! I love to dance alone, but every time I'm out there by myself, someone approaches me and asks if I'd like to dance. I don't mind dancing with one of them every now and then; foreigners dance well, so it's a lot of fun. But sometimes I just like to dance by myself, or sit back and watch the foreigners perform.

A popular club here is the Pyramid in Okinawa City. It's a fun place, but it can be a dangerous one, too. One night when I was there, a fight broke out between two military guys. The police came and everything. Then, after that rape incident in 1995, the servicemen were subject to a curfew and had to leave the clubs in Okinawa City at midnight. That rape incident was terrible. You heard about it, right? I was up on the mainland at the time, but I heard relations between Okinawans and the U.S. military were strained after that. I think the black Americans on the island suffered the most since those three guys who raped the little Okinawan girl were black. It's not fair, though, to judge a whole race of people based on the actions of three of them. There are lots of nice black people on the island who shouldn't be treated badly just because of this one incident. Unfortunately, though, too many people judge a person by what he looks like on the outside, not the inside.

Maiko-san shared with me her plans for the future, including her intention to stay on the island rather than move to the mainland as many young Okinawans have been doing in the past.

Right now I'm happy in Okinawa. I'm learning a lot about island arts and traditions in my position as Miss Okinawa. In fact, I got interested in the *taiko* [Japanese drum] recently, and I'm hoping to start taking lessons in the near future. Since I became Miss Okinawa, I've started to appreciate the island more and more. Of course I've always loved Okinawan music and dance, but during the past year I've developed an even stronger appreciation for the arts here because I realize they're unique to the island. There's nothing similar on the mainland.

In the past I considered living on mainland Japan, but life is tougher there. Here in Okinawa the daily pace is pretty slow. Up there, though, it's so crowded, and people are always in a hurry to get somewhere. On the island we take things easier; we don't pay much attention to time. Okinawa is definitely a more relaxed place.

Plus, people on the mainland always seem so concerned with school and studies. In fact, some parents start their kids studying in kindergarten in order to pass entrance exams for elementary school. It's crazy! When I was a university student, I worked for a while as a home tutor for a mainland Japanese couple who had a child in kindergarten. The mother and father were doctors. They worked a lot, so they hired me to help their child study for the entrance exam. The poor kid, he used to want to play with me when I got to his house, but I had a job to do. I heard from his parents that he was also going to *juku* [cram school] for additional instruction.

Children should have a free lifestyle, time to play. They shouldn't be cooped up studying all the time. Kids in Okinawa start going to nursery school at age 3, just like kids on the mainland, but it's different from up there; here on the island we let them be free. We don't have the same sort of attitude as the mainlanders who race around trying to get their children into the best kindergartens and elementary schools, thinking that attendance at these schools will guarantee them acceptance at the best universities on the mainland.

Even though a lot of young people these days go to mainland Japan to work or study, they always seem to return to the island. They may stay in Tokyo for two or three years, but something always pulls them back to Okinawa. Even when I was on the mainland a few years ago, I never once thought about looking for a job there. But, part of that was because I had my sights set on becoming Miss Okinawa. The owner of the jewelry store in Tokyo where I was working part-time told me if things didn't go well in the pageant I was welcome back there. Even if things *did* go well in the pageant, I was still welcome to come back in the future, he said. I never seriously considered returning, though. There are some good points to Tokyo, but there's just something about Okinawa that lures me back.

I guess in the future I'd like to get married and settle down in Okinawa.

Fortunately my parents don't pressure me by saying things like, "Hurry up and get married!" But my grandmother, she's always telling me I should start thinking seriously about it. As she says, "Marriage is what makes a woman happy!"

If I did marry, my family would like to see me marry an Okinawan, not a Japanese mainlander or an American. My grandmother thinks the people in Tokyo are cold, not as friendly as the Okinawans. As for the Americans, well, we never discussed that at my house, but I don't think my parents or my grandparents would be thrilled if I married someone from the States. People like my grandmother who experienced the war seem to have strong feelings against marriages with Americans. I don't think my parents' generation feels quite the same way. I'm not sure if that's because they didn't experience the war or what. As for my family in particular, they have a lot of pride in Okinawa and would probably just like me to marry someone from the island and stay close to home. I think most of my friends' families feel similarly.

One of the things I've become a lot more conscious of, in the past year especially, is that I'm an Okinawan through and through. I mean, this might seem strange to you, but have you noticed that I refer to myself by my first name? Okinawan girls do that. Instead of using the pronoun, "I," we use our first names. For example, I say things like, "Maiko did such-and-such yesterday," or something like that. On the mainland, though, people are taught from a young age to refer to themselves by the pronoun, "I." But on Okinawa, many of us refer to ourselves in the third person all the way through high school. Does it seem childish to you? It's a hard habit to break. I was conscious of it up on the mainland since I was the only one using my first name in conversation. Oh well, I might be able to shake the habit someday. But if not, that's OK. After all, *she grinned,* I'm in Okinawa!

EPILOGUE

In September 1998 I met with each of the nine women in this book one last time. Our meetings weren't formal interview sessions but, rather, informal visits designed to exchange good-byes and addresses.

We met at the same venues where we conducted our original interviews throughout the year: the A&W restaurant, offices in downtown Naha, private apartments, and the dance *dōjō* in the central part of the island. What distinguished these meetings from previous ones was the absence of a tape recorder, notepad, and pen. No longer was my relationship with these women one of interviewer to subject; it was suddenly one of woman to woman, friend to friend.

We began by discussing new developments in the women's lives since our last encounters. Some, such as Maiko Sunabe, experienced career changes. In July 1998 her reign as Miss Okinawa came to a close. After gracefully passing the crown to her successor, Maiko-san embarked on a bright new career with Ryukyu Broadcasting Corporation in Naha.

Others, such as Junko Isa, shared stories and photographs from a recent trip to Brazil, where she traveled to attend her nephew's wedding. Her nephew is the son of her younger sister, the only other member of Isa-san's family to survive the Battle of Okinawa. "How could I not go? They're the only family I have," she said.

Despite differences in conversational topics among the nine women, one theme remained consistent throughout our final discussions: a return to the past. Each of these women commented on some element of our previous discussions and expounded on it. Whether intentional or not, their comments provided closure to the book, an opportunity for them to furnish some final remarks about their lives. These remarks helped me decipher more about each woman's character and learn how her personal life experiences have shaped her thoughts and perspectives.

One of the major themes that is woven into these nine women's narratives is the relationship between Okinawans and Americans. Since the conclusion of World War II, the island of Okinawa has hosted a large U.S. military presence. The Americans formally occupied the island from 1945 to 1972, twenty-seven years during which they transformed the region from a rural backwater into the "Keystone of the Pacific," the U.S. military's stronghold in Asia. During these three decades of occupation, the Americans extended their powerful influence over all aspects of island life, from politics and performing arts, to food and fashion.

Then, in 1972, a new era in Okinawa's postwar history began. On May 15, the island reverted to Japanese jurisdiction, bringing the formal American military occupation to a close. U.S. troops did not disappear from the island, though. In accordance with the Security Treaty signed between Japan and the United States, they stayed behind to provide safety and stability in the Asia-Pacific region. Today, fifty thousand U.S. military personnel and their dependents are stationed on Okinawa, an island with 1.3 million inhabitants and 1 percent of the land area of Japan.

The fact that Okinawa hosts 75 percent of all U.S. troops based in Japan is particularly galling to the islanders. Why doesn't mainland Japan accept responsibility for hosting a larger portion of these facilities? the islanders plead. After all, the entire country benefits from the security the U.S. military presence provides. Tokyo remains reluctant to accommodate the Okinawans' request, however, blaming both lack of space and public resistance on the main islands. So, the bulk of U.S. troops remain on Okinawa, a reminder to the islanders of their country's loss in battle and the price that Okinawa continues to pay for that defeat.

On a personal level, how do Okinawans feel about resident U.S. military personnel? Do they appreciate, or resent, their presence on the island? From my observations I discovered that their attitude is ambivalent. Some hold the foreigners in high regard, thankful for the existence of the military bases and the economic advantages they provide. Others harbor resentment. Loss of family land, the persistence of deafening noise from military aircraft, and the frequency of crimes committed by military personnel contribute to negative sentiment. Still others, like Mitsuko Inafuku, try hard to remain neutral. After all, she was able to make a living in the immediate postwar years thanks to a job on one of the U.S. bases. And her mother was able to support herself with money from the lease of her private land to the American military. "Well, the bases are a bit noisy," she concedes. "But things here could be worse."

Based on discussions with other Okinawans, both male and female, young and old, I discovered that Inafuku-san's position is popular. I daresay it's the norm. It's difficult not to feel some sense of inconsistency on Okinawa; social, political, and even familial pressure to support or condemn the U.S. military presence is weighty, so heavy that many people find the easiest thing to do is to remain nonpartisan.

In September 1995, though, it was difficult for Okinawans to maintain their neutrality. At eight o'clock on the evening of September 4, three U.S. servicemen abducted a 12-year-old Okinawan girl, driving her to a remote area of northern Okinawa where they beat and raped her. The crime provoked outrage among the native population toward the resident U.S. military presence. Both supporters and opponents of the U.S. military condemned the act as heinous, a deplorable display by members of an organization stationed on the island to provide protection, not to sow fear.

What generated even more disgust toward the crime was the insensitivity demonstrated by Admiral Richard C. Macke of the U.S. Navy who suggested the episode could have been avoided had the three assailants hired a prostitute. He is quoted as saying, ". . . for the price they paid to rent the car, they could have had a girl."[1]

Islanders such as Fumiko Nakamura were appalled by the incident and grew more convinced that the U.S. military presence on Okinawa needs to be withdrawn. On October 21, 1995, she — and 85,000 other supporters — participated in the "Okinawan People's Rally" in Ginowan City to denounce the reprehensible crime committed by the U.S. servicemen and to demand a revision of the Status of Forces Agreement (SOFA), the legal basis for the American military presence in Japan. Formerly, the agreement granted the U.S. military custody of Americans accused of crimes until Japan formally issues an indictment against them. Once indicted, the perpetrators are handed over to the Japanese authorities. Extreme public discontent over this provision of the SOFA, however, resulted in a minor revision. From now on, if requested by the Japanese, U.S. servicepeople accused of high crimes, such as murder and rape, will be turned over to Japanese authorities prior to indictment.

The media attention the rape case attracted forced both the Japanese and American governments to reevaluate the role of the U.S. military on Okinawa and to discuss ways to prevent a reoccurrence of such a tragic and embarrassing event. Following the rape, apologies were issued, a "day of reflection" was observed by the U.S. Marine Corps on Okinawa, and a monetary collection was taken to compensate the rape victim. Other concessions included changing the way in which the U.S. military conducts exercises on the island. Artillery live-fire exercises were moved from Okinawa to mainland Japan, requiring marines stationed on Okinawa to travel to places like Hokkaido — Japan's northernmost island — and Mt. Fuji in the Kanto region to train. In addition, the U.S. military declared certain bar districts on the island off limits to military personnel between the hours of 1:00 A.M. and 5:00 A.M. and prohibited the sale of alcohol at stores on base after 9:00 P.M. Many Okinawans remained dissatisfied with these measures, though, believing the only way to prevent the recurrence of such crimes is by evicting the American military presence altogether.

The women I interviewed for this book were unanimous in expressing their outrage over the rape. Social activists such as Nobuko Karimata and Mayumi Tengan made reference to the rape case when listing reasons why the U.S. military should evacuate the island. "I don't dislike the Americans," Karimata-san was quick to point out. "It's the military that I disagree with. Their presence is dangerous. Look at that rape case from 1995. . . ." Her voice trailed off. Mayumi-san, too, expressed regret over the rape incident and objection toward the large American military populace on Okinawa. In particular, she cited military training exercises as responsible for troops' combative behavior. "They're trained to be aggressive, to kill," Mayumi-san laments. "Don't you remember that rape case in 1995?"

More than any other event, the rape incident crystallized Okinawans' fears and apprehensions about the large U.S. military contingent on the island. During the fifty years following the end of World War II, accidents, disturbances, and crimes stemming from the existence of the bases have plagued the Okinawan people. The rape, though, was perhaps the most egregious of all the offenses. It lessened confidence in the American military as a protective force and heightened suspicions of U.S. troops as uncivilized and inhumane.

Incidentally, during the same year the rape occurred, celebrations marking fifty years of military cooperation between Japan and the United States were taking place. The announcement of the rape muted words of commemoration, though, replacing them with shouts of censure. Many Okinawans continue to voice their disapproval of the military presence on the island to this day. They will not stop, they insist, until peace and tranquility are restored.

How do U.S. military personnel on Okinawa feel about the island and the islanders? Are they sensitive toward Okinawan pleas for a military withdrawal? From both personal observations and discussions with military friends and acquaintances, I learned many are sympathetic to the natives' demands. "I couldn't imagine people like the Russians, for example, building bases in my backyard," one marine officer on Futenma Air Station informed me. Others are more critical of Okinawan complaints. "If we [the U.S. military] left the island, they'd lose lots of jobs," a young enlisted marine insisted. "They're better off with us here." Whether the islanders are better off with the U.S. military presence is debatable. Proponents and opponents of this theory have bandied the issue about for years. "It's in the hands of the American and Japanese governments," many rightly conclude, shrugging their shoulders in a display of resignation.

In general, I discovered that most U.S. military personnel on Okinawa make an effort to coexist peacefully with the islanders. Servicepeople help clean beaches and parks, and even participate in cultural events such as the annual tug-of-war competition in Naha in October and the dragon boat races in Itoman during the month of May. Some tutor Okinawans in English conversation, while others take lessons in Japanese, anxious to practice their foreign language skills with neighboring Okinawans. Many American servicepeople on the island have enjoyed their tour of duty so much they elect to extend for an additional year, or two. There's just something about the island, they say, that compels them to stay.

As an American civilian living on Okinawa, I often felt caught between the world of the Okinawans and that of the Americans. I lived alone in a rented apartment in Nishihara Town, a one-room studio in a building occupied primarily by university students. Most of my daily contact was with Okinawans, either the women in my dance class, residents in the apartment complex, or professors at the university. My contact with resident Americans on the island was limited. As a civilian I wasn't able to enter the bases unescorted, thwarting my selfish desire to access the libraries, shops, and clubs that the military frequented.

I eventually met some military personnel who kindly chaperoned me onto the bases. The juxtaposition of life outside the silver metal fence with life inside it was overpowering. Narrow city streets miraculously expanded into American-style highways; concrete apartment structures transformed into houses with spring-green lawns; and cramped public spaces in town unfolded into spacious parks and recreation areas where American families picnicked and played. Traveling through the base, I had to stop and think about where I was. It was hard to believe this could exist in the middle of Okinawa, Japan, a place I once imagined as covered with nothing but sugarcane fields and stretches of caramel-colored beach.

Fumiko Nakamura remembers the Okinawa of my imagination. She grew up on the island long before it became crowded with tourist resorts and military installations. Like most islanders of her generation, Nakamura-san is waiting for the day when Okinawa is returned to the Okinawans. Only at that time, she believes, will the island revert to the peaceful place it once was.

If the relationship between the Okinawans and the Americans is difficult to describe, the relationship between the Okinawans and the mainland Japanese is equally complex, as the women in this book indicate. Though geographically a part of Japan, Okinawa has been treated inferiorly for centuries. Its secondary status vis-à-vis Japan proper has resulted in feelings of resentment, disillusionment, and deception among Okinawans, especially among those who remember World War II and the island's reversion to Japan in 1972.

World War II destroyed Okinawan faith in the Japanese military and the national government. By staging a battle on Okinawa to forestall an American advance on the main islands, Japanese troops willingly sacrificed the serenity of the island and permanently altered its landscape.

For many Okinawans, the arrival of Japanese soldiers on their soil in 1944 signified protection from approaching enemy invaders. For others, the appearance of these armed warriors signaled something quite different: an opportunity for the mainland Japanese to assert their hegemony over the islanders once again. Though some Japanese soldiers are known to have been charitable toward the Okinawans during the battle, many were notorious for committing egregious acts of cruelty and violence against their fellow countrymen. Fearful that English-speaking islanders were working as spies for the American military, the Japanese soldiers killed them. Ironically, hundreds of civilians lost their lives to the *yūgun* (friendly Japanese forces) during the Battle of Okinawa, while others were spared by American GIs. As one Okinawan woman with whom I spoke confessed, "If the Japanese had won the war, we Okinawans would be in pretty bad shape now."

Japanese treachery during wartime was not the only factor that complicated Okinawans' feelings toward those living on the main islands. *Fukki*, or reversion, in 1972, was another disappointment.

Reversion was an artificial victory for the Okinawans, an ersatz political success that brought about few real changes to the island. Those Okinawans who had hoped for a removal of the U.S. military bases, and immediate acceptance by the mainland Japanese, were disillusioned. They discovered that the end of the island's twenty-seven-year period of American Occupation and its subsequent return to Japanese jurisdiction resulted in neither a removal of the U.S. military bases that cover the island nor in unquestioning acceptance by mainland Japanese. Discrimination continued, and economic and social disparities between the main islands and Okinawa persisted.

These inequities stir the rancor of older Okinawans especially. The younger generation of islanders, those who have no recollection of war or reversion, are less severe. More willing than their parents and grandparents to accept and excuse, young Okinawans regard the mainland and its citizenry with a mixture of admiration and respect. Fascinated by the prosperity of the main islands and the economic opportunities that exist there, many of these young Okinawans over the years have headed north to study or work. People like Mayumi Tengan recall the feeling of exhilaration at moving away from Okinawa for the first time. It was freedom, she reminisced, freedom from a tiny island environment to life in an exciting new place where one could go unrecognized.

But not for long. Like many other Okinawans who spent time on the mainland, Mayumi-san, too, became a source of fascination for those around her. The mainland Japanese questioned her about Okinawa, inquiring whether the islanders wore shoes or if they could speak standard Japanese. Mayumi-san interpreted their remarks as curiosities, innocent questions from people who knew little about life on this remote Japanese island. These days, though, the effects of multimedia and tourism have increased mainlanders' knowledge of Japan's southernmost prefecture. Hopefully this knowledge will translate into a deeper appreciation of Okinawan culture and a better understanding of its sad history.

One of the saddest parts of Okinawan history is the way in which the islanders' cultural identity has been challenged over the years. As their personal narratives demonstrate, these women hold great pride in their identity as Okinawans. Eager to distinguish themselves from their mainland counterparts, many use the term *uchinanchu*, or "Okinawan" in island dialect, to emphasize their uniqueness.

The islanders were not always so eager to distinguish themselves from the mainland Japanese, though. In the years preceding reversion in 1972, Okinawans struggled to identify with the mainlanders. They waved *Hinomaru* flags and referred to themselves as "Japanese," a term brimming with nationalistic sentiment. As Tatsuko Yamada recalls, "We thought that reuniting with the main islands meant we'd finally be accepted as true Japanese." She remembers the protests against the American military presence and concurrent campaigns for return to the motherland, Japan. When reversion did not bring about the changes the islanders had hoped for, they began to take pride in their own island heritage once again.

Years of discrimination at the hands of the mainland Japanese did not permanently destroy Okinawans' pride in their identity. Traditional Okinawan dance, music, and *hōgen*, the indigenous island dialect, have enjoyed a revival in recent years, with new interpretations of old dances and island music contributing to their contemporaneity and popularity. Many interpret the resurrection of traditional arts and the popularity of *hōgen* as manifestations of the islanders' interest in remaining distinct from the mainlanders. In my opinion, they have succeeded. One moment on Okinawa and the visitor realizes the island is a special place. The music, the costumes worn at festival, the religious celebrations, and the cuisine are so different from those on the main islands that it is hard to imagine one is in the same country. Like the ocean separating Okinawa from the main Japanese islands, the differences are wide and deep.

When asked how the women of Okinawa differ from their mainland counterparts, the nine women interviewed for this book were eager to talk. They emphasized such factors as their sense of independence and their determination to change elements in Okinawan society that are deleterious to women. Frustrated with social mores of the past that dictated females should stay at home, Okinawan women are speaking out against tradition and striving to create a new, more egalitarian Okinawan society — one in which men and women participate jointly in child rearing and household duties.

Naha's Women's Comprehensive Center, headed by Nobuko Karimata, is one place on the island committed to achieving a gender-free society. Its aim is to increase awareness among men and women of problems that stymie the advancement of fair and equal gender relations on the island. Recognition of injustices in contemporary Okinawan society, Karimata-san emphasizes, is one of the first steps toward resolving them.

The Okinawan women whom I encountered during my year on the island are courageous and resourceful individuals. Many of them insist that the island's history of domination, subjugation, and occupation by a foreign power is responsible for their self-sustaining character. During World War II, they single-handedly supported their families while their husbands, fathers, and brothers protected the country. And in the aftermath of war, they succeeded in preserving the family unit and in safeguarding cultural rituals and traditions unique to Okinawa. If not for women, many Okinawans admit, the island would not have recovered as rapidly in the postwar period as it did. And many of Okinawa's traditional arts would have risked extinction.

Defying stereotypes of Asian females as tractable and acquiescent, the Okinawan women I talked to are confident in their ability to exist independent of male support. Many of the island's women are employed outside the home. This provides them with a means of economically supporting themselves while psychologically satisfying their desire for self-sufficiency. As Masayo Hirata tells us in Chapter Five, fewer mainland Japanese women have this luxury. Most are responsible for managing the household while their husbands work outside the home. And because they are dependent on their husbands for financial support, they are more likely to tolerate a poor marriage than to risk a single lifestyle. This, Mariko Higa suggests, saps women of their sense of self-worth, reducing them to subservient status vis-à-vis their husbands. Ultimately this deflates their self-confidence and courage, leaving them restless and displeased.

I would like to believe that the women whose stories appear in this book are representative of all Okinawan women. In other words, that the majority of Okinawan females are interested in social and political issues affecting them and are willing to work at changing those elements in society that thwart their advancement. There is the possibility, though, that the women whom I interviewed were uncharacteristic, uncommonly outspoken and intelligent individuals whose opinions and beliefs are different from many in society. For the most part, the nine women in this book are educated females from middle- and upper-class families. Undeniably, their opinions and beliefs will differ from other females based on their education, background, and opportunities. I am confident, though, that the foundation of their beliefs — gender equality, social and political advancement for women, and rejection of discrimination both at home and in the workplace — are common to most Okinawan women.

Several months have passed since I returned to the States from Okinawa. Admittedly, I miss "The Rock," as the island is sometimes called. It's not just the beauty of the sun-drenched beaches or the cerulean blue of the sky that beckons me back. It's also the memory of the islanders — their warm hospitality, their welcoming nature, and their willingness to share their memories of the past with me.

Sometimes I pull the cardboard box of cassette tapes from under my bed and listen to the voices of the nine women interviewed for this book. It's difficult to describe the emotion I feel. On the one hand, I am overwhelmed by a sense of nostalgia, a powerful desire to return to the island and reacquaint myself with the nine women who touched my life in such a profound way. On the other hand, I want to preserve my memories of the island the way they are; to leave them unadulterated from the effect that time and circumstance will have on them.

Naturally when I said good-bye to these nine women on Okinawa, I did so with reluctance. After all, I had no idea when I might meet with them again. But I remembered the phrase Okinawans say to one another at moments of departure. "Here on the island we don't say good-bye," they told me. "Instead we say, 'Until we meet again.'"

And so I leave you, the reader, with similar words. This is not the final book of its sort on Okinawa; we will meet the topic again. At this moment in history, the island is undergoing tremendous social and political change, changes that deserve to be watched carefully. What will happen to the U.S. military bases on Okinawa in the coming years? How will the island be transformed following a U.S. withdrawal? And what measures will be taken to improve the social and economic situation on Okinawa following an American evacuation?

This book is not the definitive resource on the topic of Okinawa. Nor is it an exhaustive study of life on the island during the war and in its aftermath. Instead, it is a piece of literature designed to introduce readers to an island and a group of people whose history has long been neglected and misunderstood. I hope this book will excite interest in Okinawa and its history and inspire more journalists and historians to pursue the topic of Okinawa in their research. After all, there are plenty of other aspects of the island that remain unexplored, and thousands of other voices that need to be heard.

AFTERWORD
MASAHIDE OTA

It is a great privilege for me to comment on *Women of Okinawa* by Ruth Ann Keyso. Not only is the writing penetrating, but Ms. Keyso writes of a subject that has been close to my heart for many years: the Battle of Okinawa, its aftermath, and its effects on the Okinawan people.

Any discussion of the Second World War and postwar Okinawa must begin with the year 1945. In that year, the Battle of Okinawa, the fiercest and bloodiest encounter between American and Japanese forces in the Pacific, was fought on our soil. Our verdant land was turned into blackened earth, and our ancient cultural heritage — our most valuable national treasure — was destroyed. One third of the civilian population perished, a number exceeding the total of American and Japanese military dead. The indelible marks of that battle continue to affect, consciously or unconsciously, every Okinawan living today.

Okinawa is both a tragic and a beautiful place. It is blessed with a rich natural environment: blue sky, blue ocean, white sand, and corals that sparkle with the colors of the rainbow. Our culture and performing arts never fail to fascinate those who come in contact with them.

It must have been that combined beauty and tragedy that lured Ruth Ann Keyso to Okinawa to write about our recent history. With insight, compassion, and clarity, she tells the stories of three generations of Okinawan women. The first are the survivors of the war, many of whom are still haunted by the thought that their lives were paid for with the blood of the dead. Theirs has been a lifelong search for meaning in the deaths of those who perished. The women of the second generation grew up during the American Occupation. They agonized over its injustices, experienced the horrors of war (during the Vietnam War) that their elders had endured earlier, and fought for Okinawa's return to Japanese sovereignty. The third are young Okinawan women caught up in the Americanization that is taking place in Asia. Our youth sport Western dress, hairstyles, and mannerisms. They have no personal memories — or far less painful ones — of the war; and the vast U.S. bases and barbed wire fences are for them a natural part of the Okinawan landscape.

As a one-time conscript in the youthful Blood and Iron Corps, and a survivor of the war, I naturally feel the closest affinity for the oldest generation. Surviving the battle by a hair's breadth, we share a common feeling that is inexplicable to others. It is a feeling of the preciousness of life that is known only by those who have leaned over and peered into the abyss called "death." Our friends and near kin are no longer alive, but they still talk to us, urging us to carry on the torch of peace so that their deaths might not be rendered meaningless. It is our sacred duty as survivors to carry on their message of peace.

In comparison, there are carefree young women of our society for whom the war has no immediacy and who freely accept the bases. The U.S. bases, as Ms. Keyso says, were "something that existed long before they were born and [for them] not likely ever to disappear." One young woman enjoys her role as Miss Okinawa; another was once fascinated by American men in jeans and T-shirts who looked like movie stars to her; yet another likes working on a military base because of the economic security the job provides for her.

We cannot blame these untroubled, lively young women. They did not see the U.S. military build-up during the war. They did not see the civilian refugees being removed to relocation camps, tiny villages, and desolate mountain areas. They did not watch base building continue even after the battle was officially over, dislodging more Okinawans from their villages and towns. After Japan surrendered, they did not see their grandparents attempt to return to their homes only to find their farmlands had been taken over by the American military.

The start of the Cold War, particularly the outbreak of the Korean War, led to the construction of U.S. bases in Okinawa at a furious pace. Fearing the loss of their means of livelihood, many Okinawans strongly resisted the seizure of their land by the U.S. military. Their farmlands, rice paddies, and village sites were taken at gunpoint. Many watched helplessly as their homes fell before the bulldozer. In utter misery, uprooted Okinawans emigrated en masse to Bolivia in search of a new way of life. Meanwhile, large American and Japanese construction firms arrived on Okinawa to expand airfields, port facilities, highways, and missile storage installations. Almost overnight, Okinawa was turned into a gigantic military base complex. Dubbed the "Keystone of the Pacific," Okinawa had central strategic importance in America's Far East defense structure.

Okinawa was now an American-occupied territory. The generation of women who grew up during the Military Occupation remember Americans as supreme authorities wielding power over the people of the island. As youngsters, they saw the bases grow larger and, as young adults, saw more GIs walk the streets of Okinawa during the Vietnam War. "Is this America or Okinawa?" they wondered. Restlessness and tension filled the air as the war raged in Vietnam. The women of this generation saw bombing runs launched from Okinawa, truckloads of GIs transported down the arterial road that was then called Highway 1, and American soldiers in Okinawa resting from the war. Not knowing whether they would live or die on their next assignment, GIs fought among themselves and robbed, raped, and murdered Okinawans. Nobuko Karimata, a prominent figure of this generation, recalls, "Those were scary years."

In all fairness, Okinawans know that the American Occupation also had a positive side. Most important, we of the older generation learned to see Americans as human beings with the same wants and loves as we had and not as the "barbarians" we had been taught to believe they were during the Pacific War. The Americans brought with them their music and art and food, the English language, and different yet interesting customs and practices. Fumiko Nakamura, a well-known peace activist, says that because of the American presence our "outlook on life has become broader, and the people have developed a more international way of looking at things." Many also feel that they have "learned a lot about American culture without ever leaving Okinawa."

But the Okinawan people began to tire of the many injustices of the American Occupation and fought hard for the island's return to Japan. Reversion finally arrived on May 15, 1972. It should have been a great turning point for Okinawa, but in practice, little changed. We Okinawans had thought that reversion would bring withdrawal of the military bases, removal of the nuclear and chemical weapons suspected of being hidden on our island, correction of the economic disparity with the mainland, and restoration of our human rights.

Today, three decades after reversion, Okinawa is still the largest American military base in the Far East. Roughly 75 percent of facilities used exclusively by the American forces stationed in Japan are concentrated here, although our prefecture represents a mere 0.6 percent of Japan's territory. The bases occupy about 11 percent of the prefecture's total area and 20 percent of the main island of Okinawa. The American forces also control twenty-nine sea areas and twenty air spaces. We are not free to use our own sea, air, or land. Our true desire is to change Okinawa from a military island into a place of peace and happiness for all people.

Article 2 of the Status of Forces Agreement, the so-called "bases anywhere formula," of the Mutual Security Treaty between Japan and the United States permits military bases to be built in any Japanese area. Why, then, should Okinawa shoulder the excessive burden? Okinawans do not want to transfer our suffering to others; however, if the Mutual Security Treaty is important for Japan, the responsibility should be assumed by all Japanese nationals. Until it is, we believe the present situation in Okinawa as discriminatory, violating the principle of equality under the law.

Discrimination brings me to the controversial period in 1996 when, as Governor of Okinawa, I refused to sign Okinawan land leases. To clarify the stand I took, let me explain what "land" means to the Okinawan people. For Okinawans, with our strong tradition of ancestor worship, land is not a mere plot of soil in which to grow crops. It is not a commodity for buying and selling. Land is an irreplaceable heritage graciously bequeathed us by our ancestors, with whom we keep strong spiritual ties. Our attachment to our land is firmly rooted, and our resistance to its forced taking is earnest.

While I was serving as prefectural governor during 1996, the Japanese Government ordered me to execute the duty delegated by the State. But I questioned the constitutionality of the Japanese Government's offering our land for U.S. military use. The Government's policy was, I believed, a violation of the rights of the Okinawan people. The forced use of Okinawan land for the U.S. military infringed on our right to own property, and the overconcentration of the U.S. military threatened our right to live peacefully. Coercing me to sign the documents ran counter to our right of self-rule — Japan's Local Autonomy Law permits a governor to deny an order issued by the central government if he feels that the order goes against the interests of the local citizenry. In this case, the central government's order clearly was not in the interests of my people. The right of property, the right to live in peace, the right of self-rule — those rights guaranteed in the Constitution for every Japanese citizen — were all I wanted for my people.

I was taken first to the Lower Court and then to the Supreme Court for refusing to sign the leases. At the Supreme Court, I sincerely requested the justices to examine the Okinawan people's plight. Denied the benefits of the Constitution, we had been living under the oppression of the military bases for more than half a century. I asked the Court to grant a judgment that could have opened up a future filled with broad possibilities for Okinawa, a future that would bring dreams and hopes for our children and our children's children. But, sadly, my plea fell on deaf ears.

Finally, let me say that although many of us protest against the U.S. bases, we are not anti-American. Fumiko Nakamura speaks for all of us when she says, "I like the Americans as individuals. It's the military I disagree with."

MASAHIDE OTA

Because of our burden and anguish, we have a very strong longing for peace. We are dedicated to a way of life that abhors and shuns armed conflict. We Okinawans are greatly troubled by having become, against our wishes, participants in the killing and maiming of other people. We did so by hosting military bases on Okinawa, from which American forces have been deployed for operations in the Korean, Vietnamese, and Persian Gulf wars.

Wars continue to be waged, and the lives of many continue to be sacrificed in places around the world. I ask today the same questions I started asking more than a half-century ago: "What is a war for? Who and what are we defending from whom?" It is my hope that all military actions will cease, and with it, the need for these disturbing questions can stop — if not in my lifetime, some day soon. Publication of this admirable book will surely hasten the coming of that day.

MASAHIDE OTA
President, Ota Peace Research Institute
Translation by Mrs. Marie Yamazato

NOTES

INTRODUCTION

1. The Ryukyu Islands comprise an archipelago that stretches southwesterly from Kyushu — the southernmost of Japan's main islands — to Taiwan.

2. Throughout this book I introduce Japanese names in Western format — the given name followed by the family name. Subsequent references follow Japanese format — the family name followed by the suffix *san*, which translates as Mr., Mrs., Miss, or Ms. This is a customary demonstration of respect in Japanese. I make an exception in Part III, when I attach the suffix *san* after the first name of each of the women — Mariko, Mayumi, and Maiko. I call them by their first names to reflect the more casual relationship our similarity in age allows. Most people in Japan refer to their contemporaries this way.

CHAPTER ONE. JUNKO ISA

1. Shuri is located 6 kilometers east of central Naha, the capital of Okinawa. It is the oldest city on the island, and was the imperial capital during the days of the Ryukyu Kingdom. During the war, no other city or village on the island had been destroyed as thoroughly as Shuri.

2. Itoman is a city located 13 kilometers south of Naha on the western coast.

3. In March 1945, U.S. intelligence determined that there were four operational airfields on the main island of Okinawa — Naha, Kadena, Yontan, and Machinato (Roy E. Appleman et al., *Okinawa: The Last Battle* [Tokyo: Charles E. Tuttle Co., 1948], 16).

4. Also known as Suicide Cliff, Kyanmisaki (Kyan Point) is located at the southern tip of the island along the East China Sea coast. During the final days of war, many Okinawans who were unable or unwilling to commit suicide by other means jumped from the cliffs into the ocean.

5. Gushikawa City is located 11 kilometers from the landing beaches of Chatan on the western coast of central Okinawa.

CHAPTER TWO. MITSUKO INAFUKU

1. *Tabi* is traditional Japanese footwear. These stiff cotton socks have padded soles and a split toe.

2. Osaka is the capital of Osaka Prefecture, one of the country's largest industrial centers. Located in the Kansai region of the mainland, Osaka is crowded with steel mills, automobile and chemical production plants, and shipbuilding factories. The city was leveled during World War II but was quickly rebuilt in the postwar period, becoming, once again, a major manufacturing and business center.

3. The mother to whom Inafuku-san refers throughout the text was not her biological mother but the woman who raised her. Her biological mother and father had six children, but her father's elder brother and his wife didn't have any, so she and her younger brother entered their home as adopted children. This was a common practice on the island in the prewar years.

4. Nagoya is the capital of Aichi Prefecture located in the Tokai region of the Japanese mainland. It is Japan's fourth largest city and is situated between the large metropolitan areas of Tokyo and Osaka.

5. Ginowan City is located in the south-central part of Okinawa, 15 kilometers north of the capital, Naha.

6. Thirty-nine thousand Okinawan men were conscripted by Japan during the war, of whom one-third were used as laborers, and twenty-four thousand as soldiers in the Home Guard (George Feifer, *Tennozan* [New York: Ticknor & Fields, 1992], 104).

7. Throughout this chapter, I calculate sums using an exchange rate of 125 yen to the U.S. dollar, the present rate at banks in Japan.

CHAPTER THREE. FUMIKO NAKAMURA

1. Emperor Mutsuhito (Meiji) was the 122nd emperor of Japan. He was born in Kyoto on November 3, 1852 and died July 30, 1912. Under Meiji, Japan transformed itself into a global power. Emperor Showa (Hirohito) was the 124th emperor of Japan. He was born April 29, 1901 and died January 7, 1989. The sitting emperor during World War II, Hirohito (Showa) was the last emperor to uphold the Shinto idea of imperial divinity.

2. Motobu Peninsula is located on the far northwestern coast of the island, about 90 kilometers north of Naha, the capital.

3. Before Japan became embroiled in war with the United States in 1941, it was already tangled in conflict with China. In September 1931, Japanese soldiers in Manchuria blew up a section of railroad and blamed the incident on the Chinese. Then they brought in troops and prepared to control the region, in anticipation of their full-scale invasion of China six years later. In July 1937, fighting erupted between the Chinese and Japanese near the Marco Polo Bridge in northern China, signaling the beginning of war between the two countries. The Japanese often refer to World War II as the Fifteen Years War, using the Manchurian Incident in 1931 as the starting point, and surrender in 1945 as the war's conclusion.

4. The Chinese calendar system (*eto*) is represented by twelve animals: *ne* (rat), *ushi* (cow), *tora* (tiger), *u* (hare), *tatsu* (dragon), *mi* (serpent), *uma* (horse), *hitsuji* (sheep), *saru* (monkey), *tori* (cock), *inu* (dog), and *i* (boar).

5. Yokohama is a Japanese port city located 30 kilometers south of central Tokyo.

6. Tennoist education emphasizes unquestioning respect and obedience toward the Emperor (*Tennō*).

7. Kyushu is the most southerly of Japan's four main islands.

8. Kanagawa Prefecture, one of Japan's smallest prefectures, is adjacent to Tokyo. Its capital city is Yokohama.

9. Nagoya, the capital of Aichi Prefecture, is Japan's fourth largest city and one of its major industrial zones. It is located in the central part of the mainland, between the large cities of Tokyo and Osaka.

10. A Quonset hut is a prefabricated, semicylindrical building constructed from corrugated metal.

11. The term *sensei,* or teacher, is a sign of respect. It is used when referring to doctors, lawyers, schoolteachers, and instructors of various arts.

12. Kobe, the capital of Hyogo Prefecture, is a port city located in western Japan, only 20 kilometers from Osaka.

13. There were actually two helo-pads on the roof of the building that were used to shuttle the High Commissioner, the Civil Administrator, and the United States Civil Administration of the Ryukyu Islands (USCAR) staff from Hanby Field, Zukeran, to the government office in Naha. Though the American flag flew from a pole on the roof, there was no visible sign that the building also housed the Chief Executive of the Government of the Ryukyu Islands, a position held by an Okinawan (Gordon Warner, *The Okinawan Reversion Story: War, Peace, Occupation, Reversion.* [Naha: Bank of the Ryukyus International Foundation, 1995]), 131).

14. The function of the Okinawa *Fujin Rengōkai* [Women's Association] during wartime included supporting the war effort by making *senninbari* for men preparing to head off to battle, cheering soldiers on as they departed for the front lines, and participating in funerals for soldiers who did not survive the war. In the postwar period, local *Fujin Rengōkai* concentrated on peaceful pursuits such as supporting the education of children, improving the status of women in Okinawan society, and strengthening community welfare programs.

15. The *Ichi Feet* Movement was established on December 8, 1983. The date was chosen deliberately: It is the same month and day that Japan attacked Pearl Harbor in 1941. The founding members of *Ichi Feet* felt the date was appropriate since it signaled the beginning of the war between Japan and America, and the Battle of Okinawa signaled the end.

16. Throughout this chapter, I calculate sums using an exchange rate of 125 yen to the U.S. dollar, the present rate at banks in Japan.

17. Okinawa shares a special relationship with people in certain South American countries such as Bolivia, Peru, and Brazil, where many Okinawans emigrated during the Meiji period (1868–1912) and again after World War II when they had no food or land and moved elsewhere to rebuild their lives.

18. Nakamura-san is referring to the rape of a 12-year-old girl by three U.S. servicemen in September 1995 on the northern part of the island. See Andrew Pollack, "Rape Case in Japan Turns Harsh Light on U.S. Military," *New York Times,* 20 September 1995, A3.

19. The Meiji era, named after the Meiji Emperor, lasted from 1868 to 1912.

CHAPTER FOUR. TATSUKO YAMADA

1. The term *sensei,* or teacher, is a sign of respect. It is used when referring to doctors, lawyers, schoolteachers, and instructors of various arts.

2. Ishikawa Village is located on the western coast of central Okinawa.

3. The *Daily Okinawan* was a 4-page tabloid military newspaper established in 1946.

4. A *bentō* box resembles a lunch box with several different compartments for items such as rice, vegetables, and fish or meat.

5. This was the origin of the Okinawan Performing Arts Federation under the direction of Chosho Goeku.

6. The *kagiyadefu* (also *kajadifu*) is an auspicious dance customarily performed as the first item in programs presented on festive occasions. It falls under the genre of elderly people's dances *(rōjin odori)*, the theme of which is the celebration of longevity and a plentiful progeny. During the age of the Ryukyu Kingdom, it was frequently performed before the king *(Ryukyuan Dance* [Naha: Okinawa Dept. of Commerce, Industry, and Labor, 1995], 27).

7. The Japanese alphabet consists of kanji characters as well as two kana syllabaries: hiragana and katakana. *Hiragana* is the cursive syllabary while *katakana* is the square form of the hiragana characters.

8. A *juku* is a Japanese cram school, an institution that provides additional instruction to students in such subjects as Japanese, math, and English among others. Many Japanese students attend *juku* in the evenings after regular classes are finished.

9. The first classical dancers to perform before public audiences were male. During the five centuries following the establishment of formal diplomatic relations between China and the Ryukyu Islands in 1404, a party of envoys from China was sent regularly to Okinawa to authorize the accession of each new king. The Ryukyu government was responsible for entertaining these men during their stay on the island and did so through the medium of dance. The ships that carried the Chinese to Okinawa were known as "crown ships" or *kwanshin,* and so the dances performed for the visitors eventually became known as "crown ship dances" or *ukwanshinudui (Ryukyuan Dance,* 8).

10. *Eisa* is a dynamic, spirited dance intrinsic to the midsummer festival, *Obon,* or the Festival of the Dead. It is a circular dance performed by both men and women (there are exceptional cases where the dance is performed solely by men or by women in certain locales) and is accompanied by the music of the *sanshin,* large barrel drums, and hand drums. Although regarded today as entertainment, *Eisa* originally had a religious function of giving repose to the dead, the dance equivalent of a memorial service for the ancestors *(Keys to Okinawan Culture* [Naha: Okinawa Prefectural Government, 1992], 37).

11. Sendai is the capital of Miyagi Prefecture, located in the Tohoku (northeastern) region of mainland Japan.

12. Yaeyama is one of the Ryukyu Island chains located southwest of the main island, Okinawa.

13. Restaurants and bars that the Occupation forces found suitable for U.S. GIs and their dependents were marked with an "A" for "approved."

CHAPTER FIVE. MASAYO HIRATA

1. ANPO is the abbreviated form of *Nichi Bei Anzen Hoshō Jōyaku,* or Treaty of Mutual Cooperation and Security between Japan and the United States of America. This treaty was signed on January 19, 1960, in Washington, D.C., and ratified on June 23 of the same year. Its ten articles stipulate, among other things, economic cooperation between the United States and Japan, cooperation with the United Nation's goals, joint defense between the United States and Japan in the event of a military attack on Japan, and permission for the United States to construct military bases on Japanese soil. The treaty has been modified over the years, the most significant modification involving Japan's ob-

ligation to assist the United States in the event of an attack on U.S. military bases in Japan (article five). Many people have criticized this condition of the treaty, referring to it mockingly as the *Nichibei Gunji Dōmei Jōyaku,* or Treaty of Mutual Military Action between Japan and the United States of America (*Okinawa Daihyakkajiten* [*gekan*], 116).

ANPO was originally linked to Japan's peace treaty with the United States (*Tainichi Kōwa Jōyaku*) signed in September 1951 and ratified the following April. Its most controversial article was article three, which placed Okinawa under the rule of the United States, thereby allowing the United States de facto power over the administration, legislation, and jurisdiction of the Ryukyu Islands.

2. President Eisenhower planned to visit Japan to commemorate the one hundredth anniversary of U.S.–Japanese friendship in 1960, but prior to that date mass demonstrations in Tokyo opposing ANPO forced his cancellation. Instead he headed to Okinawa where he was met with both cheers and jeers. Many Okinawans lined the street where President Eisenhower's motorcade was scheduled to pass, waving Japanese flags as a way of symbolizing their desire for reversion to the home islands. There were also scores of demonstrators on the street near the Ryukyu Government Office in Naha holding abusive placards displaying such epithets as "Eisenhower the War Monger," "Down with American Imperialism," and "Yankee Go Home" (Civil Affairs Activities in the Ryukyu Islands 8(2):13, as quoted in Kiyoshi Nakachi, *Ryukyu–U.S.–Japan Relations 1945–1972* [Quezon City: Hiyas Press, 1989], 101).

3. The Diet is the Japanese parliament.

4. The United States Civil Administration of the Ryukyu Islands (USCAR) was established by the American government in 1950, replacing the American Military Government (*Beigun Seifu*), the former governmental engine that ruled Okinawa from the end of the war in 1945.

5. The divorce rate in Okinawa Prefecture is the highest in Japan. Single-mother households in Okinawa account for 5.2% of all households, 2.3 times the national rate. And divorce is the main factor in 72.3% of single-mother families, compared with 62.3% nationwide. Unwed mothers are 10.9% of all single mothers in Okinawa compared to 3.6% nationally (Terunobu Tamamori and John C. James, *A Minute Guide to Okinawa: Society and Economy* [Naha: Bank of the Ryukyus International Foundation, 1995], 68).

CHAPTER SIX. NOBUKO KARIMATA

1. Early educational associations on the island in the postwar period were formed primarily over dissatisfaction with low pay scales. One of the most lasting of these early educational associations was the Okinawa Teachers Mutual Aid Society established in 1951. Its main mission was to raise the status of teachers in Okinawa to an equal level with their counterparts on the mainland. By 1952, the group revised its agenda, shaping the association into a labor union. At the same time, they changed their name to the Okinawa Teachers Association (OTA) (Gordon Warner, *The Okinawan Reversion Story* [Naha: Bank of the Ryukyus, 1995], 169).

2. Gifu Prefecture (capital: Gifu) is located in the Chubu, or middle, region of the Japanese mainland.

3. The U.S. Marine Corps established a brothel in the village of Unten on the northern Motobu peninsula in an attempt to avoid venereal disease and to get rid of camp

followers, women who were willing to trade themselves for food. The brothel was also intended to prevent the rape of civilians (George Feifer, *Tennozan* [New York: Ticknor & Fields, 1992], 163).

4. The status of both the *Kimigayo* and the *Hinomaru* are legally vague. The terms "national flag" and "national anthem" are used liberally, but, legally speaking, neither has been recognized as an official symbol of Japan. The *Hinomaru* is merely "a habitual practice," one that lacks legal grounding. And the *Kimigayo* is a hymn of praise to the Emperor, which directly opposes the pacifist Constitution based on citizen's sovereignty and opens the way for Tennoist education (Shoichi Chibana, *Burning the Rising Sun* [Kyoto: South Wind, 1992], 119).

5. At the opening of the Youth Softball Competition in Yomitan during the National Athletic Meet, Shoichi Chibana, a native of Yomitan Village, pulled the *Hinomaru* from the flagpole and burned it. He was prompted by the knowledge of what Okinawan people had suffered in recent history and of the misery of war they had experienced half a century earlier (Chibana, *Burning the Rising Sun,* 13).

6. The High School Teachers' Labor Union is known as the *Okinawa ken Kōtōgakkō Shōgaiji Gakkō Kyōshokuiin Kumiai.* It is a division of the Okinawa *Kyōshokuiinkai.*

7. Before entering the piping hot water of the Japanese bath, it is customary to shower. After soaking in the tub for ten to fifteen minutes, the bather places a heavy rubber mat over the tub to prevent the heat from escaping. The next person repeats the ritual, soaking in the same water.

CHAPTER SEVEN. MARIKO HIGA

1. At the request of the interviewee, her name and the names of other individuals in this chapter are pseudonymous.

2. Camp Kinser is one of the U.S. Marine facilities located in the southern region of Okinawa.

3. Vehicles driven by U.S. military personnel have license plates marked with a "Y" followed by a four-digit number.

CHAPTER EIGHT. MAYUMI TENGAN

1. Ehime Prefecture (capital: Matsuyama) encompasses the western and north-central coast of Shikoku, the smallest of Japan's four main islands.

2. *Obon* is the Buddhist Festival of the Dead. This festival is held during the month of August and is celebrated by gathering together with relatives at the home and offering up prayers to the spirits of the deceased.

3. Throughout this chapter I calculate sums using an exchange rate of 125 yen to the U.S. dollar, the present rate at banks in Japan.

4. Seminar House is located in Ginowan City on Okinawa Island. It is a facility with conference rooms, lodging space, and a restaurant.

5. Subic Bay Naval Base (Philippines) was one of the largest U.S. naval bases outside the United States. The base closed in November 1992.

6. There are currently 6,000 Japanese Self-Defense Forces personnel stationed on Okinawa. This compares with 28,000 American servicepeople (53,000 including dependents). The SDF operate 35 military facilities, most located in the southern region of the

main island, while the Americans control 40 facilities, of which 25 percent are concentrated in the central area of the island.

7. The total Okinawan delegation in Peking numbered seventy-two.

CHAPTER NINE. MAIKO SUNABE

1. Formerly known as Koza, Okinawa City is located in central Okinawa, 10 kilometers south of Yomitan.

2. The elephant cage is a nickname for the Sobe Communications Site run by the U.S. Navy. A giant steel ring of fencing surrounds this listening device, which was designed to eavesdrop on communications traffic for intelligence-gathering purposes. The site has also been referred to as an electronic Stonehenge. The ring measures 200 meters in diameter and 37 meters in height (Tony Barrell and Rick Tanaka, *Okinawa Dreams OK* [Berlin: Die-Gestalten Verlag, 1996], 27–29).

3. Memorial Day on Okinawa, *irei no hi,* is not formally recognized on Okinawa or mainland Japan.

4. Two hundred twenty-two students from the First Prefectural Girls Senior High School and the Okinawa Women's Normal School were mobilized during the war to work as nurses in the Japanese Army Hospital, an underground field hospital located in Mabuni Village (presently Itoman City) on the southern tip of the island. Most of the girls received training in basic medical care before beginning their jobs as nurses in January 1945. In June 1945 when they were liberated from service at the hospital, the girls fled, many losing their lives to enemy gunfire. Others committed suicide, fearful of capture by U.S. soldiers. Today there is a monument at the site dedicated to the girls who lost their lives in service to their country. This war memorial is known as the *Himeyuri-no-tō,* or the Cave of the Virgins. A peace museum is located on the premises.

5. Shimane Prefecture (capital: Matsue) is located in the Chugoku region of western Japan, bordering Hiroshima.

6. Gunma Prefecture (capital: Maebashi) is situated in the Kanto district of mainland Japan, north of Tokyo.

7. Okayama Prefecture is located in the Chugoku region of western Japan, the tail of the main island that stretches toward Kyushu.

8. An *obi* is a sash used to secure a kimono tightly around the waist.

9. Akita Prefecture (capital: Akita) is part of Japan's Tohoku region. It is the country's sixth largest prefecture and is located in the northwestern area of Honshu, Japan's main island, on the Japan Sea coast.

10. *Sanshin* (three-stringed Okinawan musical instrument) are covered in snakeskin. The prefectural tree is the Ryukyuan pine.

11. Kanazawa, the capital of Ishikawa Prefecture, is famous for its artistic legacy. The most well-known sight in the area is Kenroku-en, one of Japan's most beautiful gardens. Ishikawa Prefecture is located in the Chubu region of Honshu, Japan's main island, along the Japan Sea coast.

12. The legal driving age in Japan is 18.

EPILOGUE

1. Eric Schmitt, "Admiral's Gaffe Pushes Navy to New Scrutiny of Attitudes," *New York Times,* 19 November, 1995, A14.

GLOSSARY OF JAPANESE WORDS

anma: mother (Okinawan dialect)

banzai: a patriotic Japanese cheer, similar to "hurray!"

bentō: traditional Japanese boxed lunch

bingata: a stencil-dyed fabric of Okinawa

bōeitai: Home Guard; Okinawan men who were conscripted to defend the island during the war

butsudan: Buddhist altar

daikon: radish

danson johi: the exaltation of men and oppression of women

dōjō: an exercise or training hall; dance studio

dōri: street

doru bako: dollar box

eisa: a spirited dance performed by both men and women during the *Obon* (Buddhist Festival of the Dead) season

enjokōsai: the system whereby young teenage girls provide sexual services to older men in return for cash or gifts

enkai: party, banquet

fukki: reversion; this term is used in its political sense to refer to Okinawa's return to Japanese jurisdiction on May 15, 1972

fukki undō: campaigns for reversion

furoshiki: a large scarf used for packing and carrying goods

genkan: entrance hall or vestibule of a home, building, or school

geta: traditional Japanese wooden sandals

gobō: burdock; a coarse, weedy plant

gohan: rice

goya: a bitter, green root used in Okinawan cooking

heitai: soldier

heiwa: peace

hikokumin: traitor

Hinomaru: Japanese flag depicting a rising sun

hōgen: Okinawan dialect

ihai: mortuary tablets on which the names of the deceased are written

imokuzu: a mixture of potato starch, water, and black (unrefined) sugar

inkan: a wooden name stamp

irei no hi: Memorial Day

isamashii: brave, courageous

jūbako: nest of boxes that holds festival foods

juku: an after-hours cram school; a facility where students receive additional instruction in academic courses, usually to help them pass school entrance examinations

kagiyadefu: a traditional Okinawan classical dance performed as the first item in programs presented on festive occasions, such as weddings

kamaboko: boiled fish paste

kamekōbaka: turtle shell–shaped tomb that houses the remains of the dead

kamisama: God

kenchō: prefectural government office

kenpei: military police

kichi: military base

Kimigayo: Japanese anthem

Kokusai Dōri: International Street; the main thoroughfare of the capital city, Naha

kokusaiji: international child

kokusaijin: international or cosmopolitan person

kokusai kekkon: international marriage; a marriage of people from two different cultures

kōminka kyōiku: good citizens' education

konbu: kelp; large brown seaweed

konketsuji: child of mixed blood; one born of parents from two different races

kyōiku chokugo: Imperial Rescript on Education

Kyōshokuiinkai: Teachers Association

meishi: name card; business card

moai: informal system of moneylending clubs

mochi: sticky rice cake

Monbushō: the Japanese Ministry of Education

monpe: women's work pants that are gathered tightly at the ankles

obi: a sash used to secure a kimono tightly around the waist

Obon: Buddhist Festival of the Dead

ocha: Japanese green tea

okāsan: mother

omiai: arranged marriage; formal matchmaking

omiyage: souvenirs

otoshidama: small gifts of money given to children by relatives on New Year's Day

rotengekijō: open-air theater

Ryūbū: classical Ryukyuan dance

Ryūkyū Seifu: Government of the Ryukyu Islands

sake: Japanese rice wine

-san: genderless suffix used after a person's name as a sign of respect; translated as Mr., Mrs., Ms., or Miss

sakanaya-san: fishmonger

sanshin: traditional three-stringed Okinawan musical instrument

seimei: a religious celebration held during the month of April at which time relatives gather at the family tomb to pray to their ancestors; the gathering resembles a picnic as food and drink are brought along and offered up to the deceased souls

seiza: a style of sitting that involves folding one's legs under the body and resting the heels against the buttocks

senkō: incense stick

senninbari: a soldier's good-luck belt decorated with one thousand red stitches embroidered by one thousand different women

sensei: teacher; this term is also used for professional people in positions of authority (e.g., doctors, lawyers) as a sign of respect

shibai: plays, dramatic performances

soba-ya: Japanese noodle restaurant

soroban: abacus; a frame with parallel rods of beads used for counting

tabi: traditional Japanese footwear made of cotton, with a rubber-soled base and a split toe

taiko: Japanese drum

tate shakai: vertical society, one in which there is a distinct hierarchy of position

teishu kanpaku: a domineering husband

tatami: tightly bound mats of straw used as a floor covering in traditional Japanese homes

Tennō: Emperor

Tennō Heika: His Majesty the Emperor

totome: Okinawan tradition through which a person's inheritance, including worldly possessions and *ihai*, the mortuary tablets on which the names of deceased family members are written, are passed to male offspring, generally the firstborn male son

tsubo: a measurement of 3.3 square meters

uchinanchu: a person from Okinawa (in Okinawan dialect)

uchincha: tea made from *ukon* root, a plant in the ginger family

yūgun: friendly forces; term used by Okinawans to refer to the Japanese soldiers during World War II

yukata: informal cotton kimono worn in the summer months

yuruyaka: lenient, easygoing

zōkin: cleaning cloth

SELECTED BIBLIOGRAPHY

BOOKS AND JOURNAL ARTICLES

Appleman, Roy E., James M. Burns, Russell A. Gugeler, and John Stevens. *Okinawa: The Last Battle*. Tokyo: Charles E. Tuttle Company, 1948.

Barrell, Tony, and Rick Tanaka. *Okinawa Dreams OK*. Berlin: Die-Gestalten Verlag, 1996.

Chibana, Shoichi. *Burning the Rising Sun*. Kyoto: South Wind, 1992.

Cook, Haruko Taya, and Theodore F. Cook. *Japan at War: An Oral History*. New York: The New Press, 1992.

Egami, Takayoshi. "Politics in Okinawa Since the Reversion of Sovereignty." *Asian Survey* 34 (1994): 828–40.

Feifer, George. *Tennozan*. New York: Ticknor & Fields, 1992.

Fisch, Arnold G., Jr. *Military Government in the Ryukyu Islands 1945–1950*. Washington, D.C.: U.S. Army Center of Military History, 1988.

Heine, William. *With Perry to Japan*. Honolulu: University of Hawaii Press, 1990.

Higa, Mikio. *Politics and Parties in Postwar Okinawa*. Vancouver: University of British Columbia, 1963.

Kerr, George H. *Okinawa: The History of an Island People*. Tokyo: Charles E. Tuttle Company, 1958.

Koza: Hito, Machi, Koto. Okinawa City: Okinawa Shiyakusho, 1997.

Leckie, Robert. *Okinawa: The Last Battle of World War II*. New York: Penguin Books, 1995.

Love, Edmund. *The Hourglass: A History of the 7th Infantry Division in World War II*. Nashville: The Battery Press, 1988.

Martin, Jo Nobuko. *A Princess Lily of the Ryukyus*. Tokyo: Shin Nippon Kyoiku Tosho, Co., 1984.

Miyagi, Etsujirō. "Okinawa's 20th Reversion Anniversary." *Japan Quarterly* 39 (1992): 146–58.

———. "Redressing the Okinawan Base Problem." *Japan Quarterly* 43 (1996): 27–32.

Mochizuki, Mike. "Toward a New Japan–U.S. Alliance." *Japan Quarterly* 43 (1996): 4–16.

Morris, M. D. *Okinawa: A Tiger by the Tail*. New York: Hawthorn Books, 1968.

Nakachi, Kiyoshi. *Ryukyu–U.S.–Japan Relations 1945–1972. The Reversion Movement: Political, Economic and Strategical Issues*. Quezon City: Hiyas Press, 1989.

Nakamura, Fumiko. *Watashi no naka no Taisho Showa*. Naha: Matsumoto Taipu, 1990.

———. *Heiwa e no Ganbō*. Naha: Deigo Insatsu, 1997.

Ota, Masahide. *The Battle of Okinawa*. Tokyo: Kume Publishing Co., 1984.

Ota, Masahide, ed. *A Comprehensive Study on U.S. Military Government in Okinawa.* Naha: University of the Ryukyus, 1987.

Rabson, Steve, trans. *Okinawa: Two Postwar Novellas.* Berkeley: Institute of East Asian Studies, 1989.

Sledge, E. B. *With the Old Breed.* New York: Oxford University Press, 1981.

Takamine, Tomokazu. *Shirarezaru Okinawa no Beihei.* Tokyo: Kōbunken, 1984.

Tamamori, Terunobu, and John C. James. *A Minute Guide to Okinawa: Society and Economy.* Naha: Bank of the Ryukyus International Foundation, 1995.

Warner, Gordon. *The Okinawan Reversion Story: War, Peace, Occupation, Reversion.* Naha: The Executive Link, 1995.

——. *The Okinawa War.* Naha: Ikemiya Shokai & Company, 1985.

PREFECTURAL PUBLICATIONS

Keys to Okinawan Culture. Naha: Okinawa Prefectural Government, 1992.

Okinawa no Beigun oyobi Jieitai Kichi. Naha: Nakamaru Insatsujo, 1997.

Okinawa Sengo 50 Nen no Ayumi. Naha: Okinawa Prefectural Government, 1995.

Okinawan Crafts. Naha: Okinawa Prefectural Government, 1997.

Ryukyuan Dance. Naha: Okinawa Department of Commerce, Industry & Labor, 1995.

U.S. Military Bases in Okinawa. Naha: Military Base Affairs Office of Okinawa Prefectural Government, 1997.

OTHER PUBLICATIONS

Okinawa Daihyakkajiten (jōkan, chūkan, gekan). Naha: Okinawa Times, 1983.

Okinawa Economic Factbook. Honolulu: United States Pacific Command Strategic Planning and Policy Directorate Research and Analysis Division, 1996.

The Okinawas of the Loo Choo Islands: A Japanese Minority Group. Honolulu: Office of Strategic Services Research and Analysis Branch, 1944.

Watkins, James T., IV. *Papers of James T. Watkins IV. Historical Records of Postwar Okinawa: The Beginning of U.S. Occupancy.* Ginowan: Ryokurindo Shoten, 1994.

ACKNOWLEDGMENTS

I could not have written this book without the support of the nine women whose stories appear on these pages. Throughout my year on Okinawa, they demonstrated an intense generosity of spirit and a powerful desire to share their recollections of the past with me. I truly appreciate their help, their patience, and their willingness to aid me in the production of this book.

Of course I also owe a debt of gratitude to the Ito Foundation for International Education Exchange in Tokyo for its financial support. Thank you for sensing my enthusiasm for this project and for helping me to execute my research.

I also acknowledge the people who acted as editors and consultants during the writing stage of this project, in particular Chris Ames, John Campbell, Adriane Fink, Bob Harvie, Joe Johansen, Mike Kenat, Laura Lackey, Andrew Lange, Chris Nelson, and Sheila Smith. Their insightful comments and helpful suggestions greatly improved the quality of this book. I am indebted to my brother, Andrew Keyso, Esq., too, for his legal advice and assistance.

And, of course, a very special thanks to my editor, Roger Haydon, of Cornell University Press, who believed in this project as much as I did and devoted much time and effort to getting the book published.

To the many other people who helped me get established on the island and who aided me in finding women to interview for this book, I extend my deepest appreciation. I thank Professor Takayoshi Egami of the University of the Ryukyus especially, for acting as my sponsor during my year on Okinawa.

Finally, I express my gratitude to my parents, relatives, and friends whose e-mails, telephone calls, prayers, and letters of encouragement were instrumental in helping me to complete this project.

ABOUT THE AUTHOR

Ruth Ann Keyso earned a bachelor's degree in government
from the University of Notre Dame in South Bend, Indiana, in 1991.
Following graduation she worked as an English instructor in Ibaraki
Prefecture, Japan, as a member of the Japan Exchange and Teaching
Programme (JET) sponsored by the Japanese Ministry of Education. In
1994 she was invited to teach at Kumon Leysin Academy of Switzerland, a
boarding school for Japanese high school students. Upon completion of
her master's degree at the University of Michigan's Center for Japanese
Studies in 1997, Keyso received a fellowship from the Ito Foundation for
International Education Exchange to conduct a year of private research
in Okinawa, Japan.

In December 1999 Keyso completed a master's degree in journalism at
Northwestern University's Medill School of Journalism. She resides
in the northern Chicago suburbs with her husband Mark.

❀